MOUNTAIN MAIDU AND PIONEERS

A History of Indian Valley,
Plumas County, California,
1850 - 1920

A Graduate Study Presented to the Graduate Council
Chico State College
In partial Fulfillment of the Requirements for the Degree Master of Arts
1963

PATRICIA KURTZ

iUniverse, Inc.
Bloomington

Mountain Maidu and Pioneers
A History of Indian Valley, Plumas County, California, 1850 - 1920

Copyright © 2010 Patricia Kurtz

iUniverse books may be ordered through booksellers or by contacting:

iUniverse
1663 Liberty Drive
Bloomington, IN 47403
www.iuniverse.com
1-800-Authors (1-800-288-4677)

ISBN: 978-1-4502-6175-3 (pbk)
ISBN: 978-1-4502-6176-0 (ebk)

Printed in the United States of America

iUniverse rev. date: 11/20/2010

Contents

Preface   ix

1. GEOGRAPHICAL DESCRIPTION   1

2. ABORIGINES   4

    VILLAGES, HOUSING, and CLOTHING   5
    FOODS, - GATHERING, PREPARING, and STORING   11
    TOOLS and IMPLEMENTS   16
    BASKETRY   19
    TANNING   27
    TRANSPORTATION, TRAILS, and TRADE   28
    SOCIAL PRACTICES   29
    STORIES OF CREATION and BELIEFS   31

3. FIRST WHITE SETTLERS and SETTLEMENT of INDIAN VALLEY   34

    GOVERNMENT INDIAN POLICY   37
    PEACEFUL RELATIONS   38
    INDIAN TROUBLES   40

4. MINING SETTLEMENTS   45

    TAYLORSVILLE   45
    COPPERTOWN   50
    ROUND VALLEY   50
    GREENVILE   52
    CHEROKEE   54
    WOLF CREEK   55
    ARLINGTON   55
    CRESCENT MILLS   56

5. ACCULTURATION OF THE INDIANS   62

    INDIAN MISSION   65
    END OF SOME SOCIAL PRACTICES   67

Notes   69

Bibliography   75

Appendix A   79

Appendix B   81

LIST OF FIGURES

1. Map of Study Area   3
2. Map of Indian Sites   7
3. Variations of Mountain Maidu Dwellings   9
4. Mountain Maidu Snowshoes   11
5. Hunting Equipment   18
6. Basketry Techniques   19
7. Daisy Baker Making a Basket   20
8. Examples of Coiled Baskets   21
9. Examples of Twined Baskets   22
10. Basket Collection of the Meadows Family   23
11. Examples of Wicker Baskets   24
12. Lilly and Daisy Baker Preparing Willows with Kit Kurtz   25
13. Basket Shapes   27
14. Taylor's Mill   47
15. View of Taylorsville   48
16. Snowshoes on Horses   49
17. Vernon House and Hardgrave Stage   50
18. Scene in Greenville   53
19. Main Street of Greenville   53
20. Logging in Taylorsville   56
21. Map – 1866   59
22. Copy of Keddie Map – 1892   61
23. Copy of Letter Concerning Baker Allotment to Indian Bureau   64

PREFACE

Histories of California's past have been primarily concerned with the progress, triumphs, and failures of the white population. Small segments of the state's population, the California Indians, found a place in recorded history only when they were in conflict with modern civilization. In Plumas County, Indian Valley's history followed that pattern in a lesser way. Its mineral wealth, dense forests, and beautiful landscapes have been extolled, but little was recorded about its people, white and Indian. Two early and rare volumes, History of Lassen Plumas, and Sierra Counties published by Fariss and Smith in 1882, and in 1908 The Northern Maidu by Roland B. Dixon, aided the writer and were most comprehensive sources. Gaps which remained in this history of Indian Valley were filled chronologically with evidence gleaned from letters, diaries, newspapers, and personal reminiscence of pioneers. By no means is this to be considered the complete story of Indian Valley, as there may be deposits of historical evidence yet untouched which should provide a challenge to future researchers.

This history has been interwoven with the perspective of the local Indian, the Mountain Maidu. This story has never been told in proper sequence and this paper attempts to tell a part little known to most people. The writer is indeed grateful to friends and acquaintances, both Indian and white, who have given so freely of their files, collections, books and time. Without the help of Lilly Baker, her mother Mrs. Daisy Baker, and Mr. and Mrs. Bruce Bidwell, the writer could not have attempted this research.

Chapter I

GEOGRAPHICAL DESCRIPTION

Indian Valley is located in the western part of Plumas County in the southeastern part of the northern half of California. The floor of the valley ranges from 3,480 feet to 3,600 feet above sea level and contains 16,000 acres. This is surrounded by high mountains, some over 6,000 feet. The entrances to the valley are through stream canyons, three entering the valley and one leaving it. These streams are Wolf Creek in the northwest, Lights Creek in the northeast and Indian Creek in the southeast. Wolf and Lights Creeks join Indian Creek in the central part of the valley and flow out as Indian Creek in the southwest, a branch of the Feather River (see Figure on page 3).

The valley is part of the northern terminus of the Sierra Nevada where it approaches the Cascade Range and lies between two mountain ridges, the Diamond Mountain Block and the Grizzly Mountain Block. It appears to cut across the Grizzly Mountain Block which would be continuous with Keddie Ridge were it not for the valley. The valley varies from a fourth of a mile to more than two miles in width. The main part of the valley lies in the northwest. North Arm begins at the east end and runs northerly for about four and one-half miles ending at two branches. The third extension begins in the southeast corner and is a long narrow arm that gradually broadens into Genesee Valley. It is more than nine miles in length.

The mountains which flank the valley are Keddie Ridge, with Keddie Peak, 7,499 feet high, in the northeast; Mt. Jura, 6,275 feet, on the east; Grizzly Ridge with Grizzly Peak, 7,704 feet, in the southeast; Mt. Hough, 7,232 feet, in the south; and a ridge in the west, 5,362 feet high, which bears no name but has near its summit Round Valley Lake.

An early observer in the valley wrote in 1854 in <u>Hutchings California Magazine </u>the following description:

> It is beautifully picturesque and fertile, and about twenty-three miles in length—including the arms—by six in its greatest width; being about fifteen miles southwest of the great Sierra Nevada chain; and (like most of these valleys,) runs nearly east

and west. Surrounded, as it is by high, bold, and pine covered mountains of irregular granite… This valley is well-sheltered. [1]

The valley area and part of the mountains share the plant and animal life of the Transitional Life Zone. Both broadleaf and evergreen trees grow on the slopes around the valley. These trees are oaks, maples, cedars, firs, and pines and share the slopes with dense undergrowth of manzanita and buckthorn. Stream channels are edged with willows, alders, and cottonwoods. Herbaceous plants are profuse in the spring and summer, and wild grasses, tules, and rushes cover the valley floor.

Fish abound in the streams, the dominant species being trout. The black bear and black-tailed deer are the largest wildlife and share the forest with the coyote, fox, porcupine, woodchuck, squirrel, rabbit, and weasel. Otter, beaver, and muskrat are found in the streams. Birds are represented by numerous varieties of waterfowl, birds of prey, game birds, woodpeckers, and perching birds.

Recorded observations of temperature disclose that the extremes range from a summer high of well over 90 degrees F. to well below 0 degrees F. in the winter. Although days are warm and hot in the summer, the nights are cool and pleasant. In the winter, temperature may drop well below freezing at night but is usually above freezing during the day. The relative warmth of the winter days as compared to the cold nights may be explained by elevation in that there is less dense atmosphere at high altitudes than at sea level. This thinner atmosphere allows for more rapid absorption of the sun's heat and more radiation of that heat at night.[2]

The average rainfall per annum measured at 36.8 inches.[3] Precipitation is greatest during the winter and spring months. Indian Valley lies in the belt of heavy snow and there have been winters when accumulated snows have reached the depth of five feet, although it usually averages two feet. Residents often claim that the valley is the land of two seasons, summer and winter. The spring and fall seasons have been known to be consistently short, and it is not unusual for it to snow in May and September. Hardly a summer passes without the phenomena of a brief hail or snow storm. The Indians say that if the frost gets the apple blossoms, the snow will remain on Mt. Hough and Mt. Lassen all summer long.

A picture of Indian Valley's past is enhanced by an understanding of its geographical features. For the same reason a background of the native life of the area and how it fared upon the arrival of the first settlers and thereafter is vital in understanding its history.

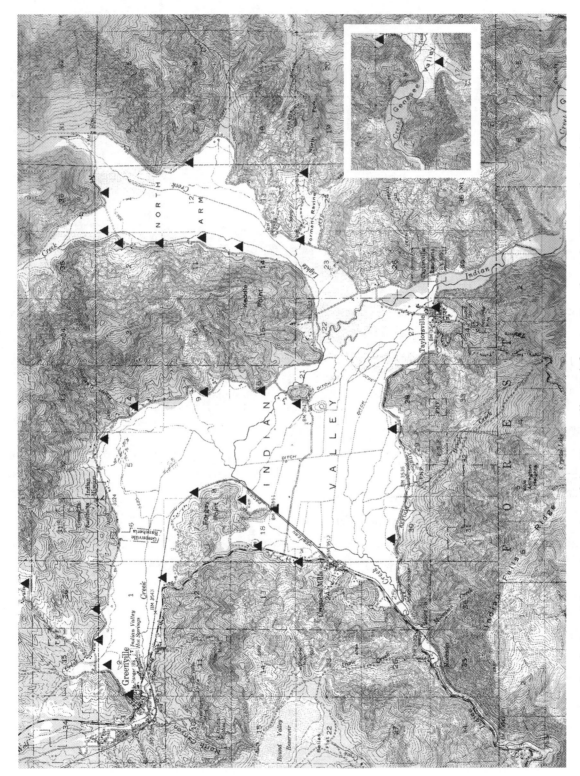

Study Area Map – A portion of the Greenville, California, Quadrangle, US Geological Survey.

CHAPTER II
ABORIGINES

The journals of J. Goldsborough Bruff provide the first written record of Indian Valley Indians. Bruff entered the valley in 1850 from the east as a member of Peter Lassen's prospecting party in search of Stoddard's Gold Lake. Some of the Indians may have encountered white men before, but their attitude was one of timidity and fear or of shy friendliness, never hostility.[1]

The first white men called the Indian Valley Indians "Diggers", a name originally given to the Shoshone of the Great Basin area and later applied to all of the Indians of California. The Indians themselves claimed that *To si dum* was their name before the arrival of the whites.[2] Stephen Powers, writing on the tribes of California in 1877, said, "they have no name of general application except they all call themselves *mai du*, (Indians) … in Indian Valley, up in the mountains, are the *To si ko ya*." [3] The name Maidu has since been applied as a tribal name for the Indians of this section of California.

The Northeastern or Mountain Maidu, which include the Indian Valley Indians, inhabited a distinct topographical area and possessed a distinctive language of their own.[4] From the linguistic viewpoint, anthropologists have placed these people in the Penutian Linguistic Family.[5] The other tribal divisions were Southern or Valley Maidu (Nisenan) and Northwestern or Hill Maidu (Konkow). The culture, customs, or habits of the Northeastern or Mountain Maidu were more like that of their northern mountain neighbors, the Atsugewi, than they were of the hill or valley relatives. The Mountain Maidu were considered the poorest of the Maidu with a culture status less advanced than their neighbors.[6]

The Maidu were called lazy and shiftless, but it is evident that this could not be true when one considers the geographical features of the area. The rigors of this physical environment, flat marshy valleys, rugged surrounding mountains, long winters, and short summers, all were factors in restricting these people to their peculiar way of life. Because of these limitations of a hostile environment, most of their energy was directed to providing themselves with basic needs. Food, shelter, and clothing were wrought from the wilderness with crude implements of stone, wood, and bare hands, but extensive knowledge was demonstrated as to how to use plants and animals for food, clothing, medicine, tools, and utensils.

Apparently there was a complete lack of any clan organization. The people were grouped loosely in village communities.[7] Land was not individually owned but was free and common to all the members of the tribal community within the valley. Hunters could search for and pursue game within their political area. Women and children shared desirable spots for the harvesting of wild crops. Their chief was chosen for his wealth and popularity and was easily deposed if he became unsatisfactory to the majority. He never received more than an average share of food. [8]

VILLAGES, HOUSING, and CLOTHING

Many village sites have been discovered in Indian and Genesse Valleys. Some of these sites have been identified as a result of yet incomplete archaeological evidence (see Figure on page 7). It was believed that the population of the valleys may have been dense, but it also seems probable that after living in one spot for years, the people moved.[9] Location of villages along edges of timbered tracts overlooking the valley showed that much thought was given as to desirability in year-'round weather. Many sites allowed for protection from summer heat and made use of winter sun. Water was abundant and ever available in numerous spring-fed streams. For a people dependent upon nature for their sustenance, these locations were practical.

Bruff stated that Indian lodges were numerous in this valley and villages probably edged the entire valley. When the white men moved in and took over the land for cultivation of crops, the Indians gradually concentrated their number in fewer and hence larger communities. The Maidu population diminished after contact with the white men and in 1899 Dixon felt that there were not over 250 full-blooded Maidu.[10] The following is a list of villages with their Indian names by both Dixon and Young: [11]

White Settlement	Maidu Village (Dixon)	(Young)
Greenville	*Ko – tasi*	*Ko – tasi*
Taylorsville	*Tasi – koyo*	*Tasi – koyo*
North Arm	*Hopnom – koyo*	*Hop – nom*
Crescent Mills		*Ku-yom-bu-ku*
Genesee	*Yotamoto*	*Yo-tum-bu-tu*

Settlements in existence upon the arrival of the white men showed no definite pattern as to the number, placement and type of dwelling in each village. The only individual characteristic was that each village had a sweat house which was inhabited as other houses. Villages of any great size usually had a dance house.[12]

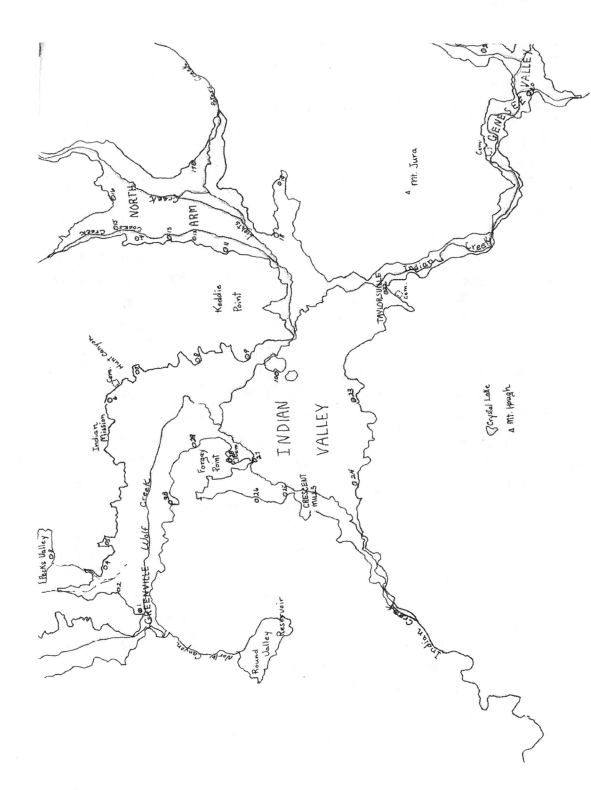

Map of Indian Valley showing locations of Indian Village sites.

A village was made up of anywhere from four to twelve houses. The settlements around Taylorsville illustrate this:

A. *Yodawi* (with the largest sweat house and one and a half miles from Taylorsville across the stream) 10-11 Houses and 1 Sweat House

B. *Ong-koyo-dikom* (three miles from Taylorsville) 4-5 Houses and 1 Sweat House

C. *Kushdu* (at Taylorsville) 6 Houses and 1 Sweat House [13]

There could have been anywhere from five to ten persons living in a house. These persons were related by blood. [14]

Two types of structures were used in building: the *k'um* was a large earth-covered structure and was a dwelling, a dance chamber, and/or a sweat house; and the *hubo* was a lean-to dwelling of bark or brush. Each village had at least one *k'um* or sweat house. It had been thought that the *k'um* was a winter habitation and the *hubo* was a summer structure. Bruff evidently thought so when he encountered these people in 1850, as notations on his sketches designate the *hubo* as a temporary shelter and the *k'um* as a winter lodge.[15] The *hubo* served as a winter dwelling for some lazy mountain people, and women indisposed used them for periods of seclusion.

The *k'um* was a round structure twenty to forty feet in diameter. It was built over a shallow pit, three feet deep, dug out with sticks and baskets by women. The side of the pit was sometimes lined with upright poles, split logs or bark. Three posts with forked tops were set upright forming an isosceles triangle around the center fireplace with the shortest side toward the entrance on the south. These rose from ten to twenty feet. Beams were then placed from the center posts to the earth sides of the excavation Cross poles were laid following the circumference of the house, then bark of incense cedar, sticks, and pine needles were put on top with a final layer of earth one foot deep (see Figure on page 9). Entrance was usually made through the smoke hole in the center of the roof. Descent was achieved on a notched log or a ladder made of two poles with cross pieces tied on with serviceberry withes. The tunnel-like door in the front served for draft, the bringing-in of wood, and an occasional entrance by women and children. At night this entrance was closed, thus shutting out the air supply and causing the fire to burn very slowly producing adequate heat for the occupants. Having the floor below ground level also contributed materially to the warmth of the *k'um*. [16]

The *hubo* was a conical frame structure, ten to fifteen feet across, built over a shallow exaction. Poles were leaned and tied together, then covered with sticks, bark and pine needles. The excavated earth was piled against the sides as far as it would go. A smoke hole was in the center. Some *hubo* had a center pole supporting the structure in the middle. Sometimes a simple doorway was achieved by setting two sticks in the ground with a cross piece at the top. A niche was built in the back for storage of food.[17]

A. Top of page: Plan of Maidu earth lodge, *k'um* (after Dixon) a. Fireplace, b. Main post with forked top, c. Front posts with forked tops.

B. (Center) Exterior view of earth lodge.

C. (Bottom) Temporary shelters of the Northeastern Maidu (after Brruff).

When several families lived in a dwelling, each family was assigned to a portion of the house, cooked its own food, and shared the fire. Floors were covered with layers of grass or woven tule mats. Inhabitants slept with feet toward the fire on bedding of deer, bear or elk skins, and woven blankets of rabbit fur strips. These were rolled up during the day and provided back rests or the only seats. At a nearby stream faces were washed by throwing cold water against the skin and saying *"Hoos-ka"*, meaning "chase away evil things." This ritual was repeated after attending ceremonies for the dead.[18]

Dress of these mountain people was scanty by present-day standards. Women wore two fringed buckskin aprons ornamented with strung pine nuts. The front one was smaller and tucked between the legs when the wearer sat down. In the winter a skin robe and moccasins were added to this costume. Hair was worn loosely and combed with a comb made out of a porcupine's tail.

The men wore a loin cloth in the summer and a mantle of deer or puma skins with the hair toward the body in the winter. Their moccasins were single pieces of hide seamed up the front and coming well above the ankle. Grass was stuffed in the moccasins for warmth in the winter. Snowshoes were necessary in this climate. They were oval in shape with three cross pieces to support the foot. Small green limbs were heated to fashion the oval frame and then wrapped with strips of buckskin, fur side down, for better traction. There was no heel play as the whole foot was bound down (see Figure on page 11). Leggings of deerskin with the hair side inward covered the calf and were worn for traveling and the hunt. Hair was most frequently trimmed with a glowing coal and old men wore a netted cap known as a *wika* made of Indian hemp. Face hair was usually pulled out, although the upper lip was left covered. [19]

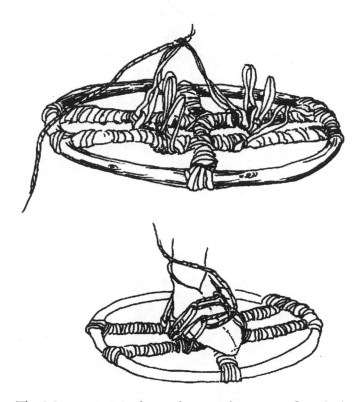

The Mountain Maidu made snowshoes out of rawhide,
buckskin and green limbs. (after Dixon).

It was observed by early settlers that some of the Maidu appeared better off than others. Some houses were better constructed than their neighbors, and some of the people themselves appeared to have been better dressed. So it was with the gathering of food, as these families too improvident to secure, prepare, and store an adequate food supply for the winter often went hungry.

FOODS, - GATHERING, PREPARING, and STORING

Acorns, *ham sim*, were the "staff of life" to the Maidu. The acorn of the California Black Oak, *Quercus kelloggii,* was preferred. When ripe in the fall, the nuts were knocked to the ground by men and boys who climbed the trees. Women and children gathered them and placed them in conical burden baskets which were carried on their backs with buckskin thongs across the shoulders.[20] Crops varied from year to year, and nuts were stored for protection against famine. Willow granaries or cribs held unprepared nuts outside the dwelling, while large round baskets stored shelled nuts in the house.

Each nut was shelled by cracking it with a rock hammer. The meats were spread in the sun and were not used until thoroughly dry. A stone mill, usually a slightly hollowed flat rock and a smaller one fitting the hand, was used to grind the meats into flour. Usually an open-bottom hopper basket, or mortar basket, held the nuts and flour in place on the slab while the grinding was in process. As the nuts were ground, the coarser meal came to the top. The meal was scooped off, sifted, and the coarse flour was returned to the mill until all was of the same fine consistency. Fine white sand was then spread evenly on the ground an inch or two in depth and hollowed slightly into a flat bowl. The acorn flour was sprinkled evenly over the sand and water was slowly poured over the meal. Leaching out the astringent tannic acid was achieved by repeating this process of pouring water over the flour many times. As this was done, the flour first became dark brown in color and turned into a semi-gelatinous dough, but eventually turned light tan. The dough was then picked up by the handful and the sand gently washed off. As the dough dried it crumbled into flour. When prepared for a meal, a piece of dough was crumbled and mixed with cold water into a cooking basket. Hot stones were taken from a fire, washed quickly in a basket of water, and tossed gently into the dough mixture. The mush would immediately begin to boil. When a stone became exhausted of its heat, it was retrieved with two sticks and replaced with a hot one. The mush was considered ready to eat when it became cohesive and dropped away from the stones. This mixture was scooped up with the index and middle fingers and sucked off. A thinner consistency, soup, was also made. Bread was made by spreading thick dough evenly around a rock and then cooking it on coals. These patties were carried by travelers and hunters for meals on their trips.[21]

Other plants provided great variety to the diet and were gathered in season from early spring through late fall. In spring, groups left their winter earthen houses and operated from temporary camps. Many miles would be traveled to good harvesting areas. During years of famine they would resort to eating the inner bark of aspen or tamarack. Herbs, roots, and bulbs were gathered in the spring along with mushrooms. These were dug with a digging stick, approximately three feet long and made of strong wood. It has been said that when the first white settlers saw the Indians digging for food with their sticks they gave them the nickname of "Diggers".

Camas bulbs, gathered early in the summer in marshy areas, were considered a sweet delicacy when roasted. Squaw potatoes, purple and white brodiaea, pink and white onions, cattails, tules, and wild carrots were other root foods available to the people of Indian Valley. These roots were eaten in numerous ways: raw, roasted, boiled; or dried, pounded finely, mixed with berries and baked in small flat cakes. [22]

The leaves of a pungent plant of the carrot family, *lop-bom*, were highly desired in the spring. It was boiled in its fresh state in cooking baskets or dried for future use during the year. Clover tops, mule-ears and cattails were eaten fresh and also baked in earthen pit ovens that dried them for winter soups. Young thistle stalks and soap-plant stems were collected when young and tender.

Sunflower seeds, *bo-kum*, of the balsam root and mules-ear were eaten after they had been parched, winnowed, ground and made into patties. These were considered a dessert.

Small seeds of grasses and other plant were gathered with beaters. These were ground with water and baked in cakes to be used in a soup similar to that of the acorn.[23]

These Indians made soup or a drink from chokecherries, elderberries, manzanita berries, or gooseberries after they had been pounded and mixed with water. Manzanita berries and gooseberries were knocked off the plants with beaters into large flat baskets. Beaters of wicker were also used in winnowing the leaves from the berries. When pounding chokecherries to remove the seeds from the pulp, this chant was repeated:

He nesk ko pem, Boo hous chgna no, Boo hous chgna no.

As translated by Lilly Baker, a northeastern Maidu, the meaning was: "eyelid, eyeball, knock it open, knock it open." This chant continued until the mixture was juicy and good enough for soup. Wild raspberries, *wi do pum*, chokecherries, *hau nau num*, and serviceberries, *so bam*, were made into patties and dried for winter use.[24]

Nuts from the cones of both the yellow and sugar pines were collected in the fall. The sugar pine nuts were the most desirable and often were used in trade with other tribes. Trees were climbed to dislodge the cones. Pitch was burned off by placing the cones on end, covering them with dry grass and then burning the grass. By pulling the scales back the nuts were easily removed from the cones.

When Mormon crickets, *li chu ae*, and locusts, *tu leem*, appeared in great numbers, they were gathered for food. This was done early in the morning when the insects were inactive. A fire was built in a pit and when it was reduced to coals the insects were dumped in, immediately covered with earth, and so cooked. When removed from the earthen oven they were allowed to dry in the sun and then stored for the winter. The heads and legs were removed and the bodies ground into flour for soup. Grubs of the yellow jackets were considered such a delicacy that the young folks were not allowed to eat them. These were dried and sometimes used in trade with other tribes. Red ant eggs and angleworms were also considered edible. [25]

Fresh water mussels were easily gathered along the edges of streams and ponds. These were steamed in the shell over coals in shallow pits. It was not unusual to see piles of burnt mussel shells around the dwellings. [26]

When passing through Big Meadows seven miles northwest of Indian Valley, in 1849, Bruff wrote the following observations about the abundance of game in the area. [27]

> Great place for deer, cracking of rifles heard in the hills and woods in every direction… Scott and his comrades returned late at night with lots of grouse, hares, etc… Numerous fish swimming about as leisurely as gold fish in a vase.

Even though Indian Valley is one thousand feet lower than Big Meadows, the environments are similar. Indian Valley is in the center of the Transitional Life Zone while Big Meadows is at the upper edge of the zone. It would be safe to assume that the

Indians of Indian Valley shared an abundance of game similar to their neighbors in the north. Rather than migrating to the foothills, deer herds wintered in Indian Valley.

In 1899, Dixon discovered in his study of the northern Maidu that their food supply included practically everything edible except wolf, coyote, dog, buzzard, lizards, snakes, and frogs. Deer, elk, mountain sheep, and bears were plentiful and smaller game such as rabbits, raccoons, and squirrels were numerous. [28]

Of all the flesh foods, deer were most numerous. Deer provided the people with many needs other than just food, and few parts of the animal went to waste. The brain was used in tanning of hides. The heart was eaten by adults, but was taboo to all children and youths. Eyes were eaten to improve eyesight. Liver, heart, entrails, and the fetus were considered edible. The vertebras were ground up and molded into small cakes and eaten dry. Blood was boiled before eating. [29] Hides provided their blankets and clothing. Other usable parts helped in the making of tools and some were primarily the tool itself: sinews in bow making; antler wedges for splitting wood; and bones for awls, scrappers, and drills.[30]

A good hunter was held in high esteem socially. Strict taboos were in force for the families of hunters. The hunter often went to great extremes to get "deer power" to possess him as it gave him skill and good luck. Tobacco was smoked ceremonially and the shaman supervised the prayers and singing. Shell beads were offered to increase the "deer power". Hunters conversed with their bows and arrows about the hunt and weapons were smoked over the fire. [31]

Men hunted individually or in groups. Lone hunters had a favorite method for hunting deer, wearing as a disguise a whole deerskin including the head antlers. With the bow and arrow held close to the chest, the hunter would approach his quarry cautiously behind bushes, imitating a buck feeding. When close enough the deer would be shot with the bow and arrow and since the arrow was silent the animal would not be startled. Sometimes the hunter could get more than one deer.[32] An individual hunter was able to trail deer for days by carrying enough food to sustain himself while moving. The animal would not get a chance to feed or rest and would gradually become weakened to the point where the hunter could get close enough to shoot. Often deer were lured when hunters blew on a leaf or grass to imitate the cry of a fawn.

Hunters in groups concealed themselves near deer licks and easily shot deer on moonlit nights. Deer were also driven past hunters strategically hidden along fences built of brush, vines, and stones. The hunters would shoot at passing animals or club them when cornered. Opportunities occurred where deer could be driven over cliffs. When hunting in groups the hunters usually divided the kill, but a lone hunter could claim his own.

After the hunt, the hunters participated in cleansing ceremonies along with the division of the meat. A youth was switched with a bow string after killing his first game. To return without meat was a disgrace.[33]

The Indians prepared meat of large animals by first skinning the animal and then roasting the carcass in a pit. The pit was lined with rocks on which a fire was built. When the rocks were thoroughly heated, all debris was removed and the carcass was placed in the pit on a layer of green pine needles. Large heated rocks were then put in the body cavity with smaller hot rocks wedged around it after the legs had been tied together. Layers of pine needles were spread over the animal completely covering it, followed by layers of dirt and hot ashes. Roasting time took from several hours to half a day.[34] When the meat was to be preserved for winter use, the men would cut the fresh and raw carcass into pieces which could be handled by the women. The women then cut the meat into narrow strips and hung them on wooden frames to dry in the sun or over a fire. This jerked meat was stored in large baskets and later eaten in the dry form or cooked with acorn mush.[35]

The Maidu hunted black bears, *moo dum*, when they were hibernating. Pitchy torches placed in front of the den entrance eventually smoked the bear out. He was then shot at close range while still in a stupor. Bear meat was cooked separately from deer and the two were never eaten together. Fresh bear blood was thought to make a man very healthy forever, if the man were strong enough to drink it in the first place. A weak man would be promptly killed if he drank it.

Grizzly bears, *pa nom*, were larger and more aggressive than the black bear. Hunting them with a bow and arrow was dangerous because the wounded animal was extremely ferocious. A lone hunter lured the beast along a trail where numerous hunters had been carefully posted. As the animal was lured the hidden hunters would shoot at the bear with the hope that it would soon succumb to their numerous arrows. [36]

Small animals hunted by the Indians of Indian Valley included raccoons, skunks, badgers, porcupines, rabbits, squirrels, gophers, and woodchucks. They also sought birds – eagles, hawks, ducks, geese, swans, grouse, quail, pigeons, woodpeckers, blackbirds, robins, and numerous other species.

Rabbits driven into long nets made of Indian hemp or milkweed fibers became entangled and were clubbed to death. Carefully manipulated stone and log deadfalls fell on small animals when traveling on well used runways. Some of these deadfalls were triggered with baited lines. Earth-dwelling animals were smoked or dug out of their burrows. In setting nooses and snares for small animals, the natives cleverly arranged bent tree limbs to provide the power of the trap. Some of these animals may have been shot with untipped arrows and slings.

During migrations of waterfowl, the Indians set traps so that the birds would become entangled when forced to take off from the water. Geese caught early in the summer were unable to fly and were used as live decoys to help capture others under a row of nets. Similar nets held lightly by a leaf snared ducks in the dark. Children searched for eggs of waterfowl and eggs of other species were also taken for food when found.

Since rabbit skins were used for the making of blankets, these people skinned the rabbits before they were cooked. However, other small animals were roasted on a single stick over hot coals. Should a traveler have the opportunity to make a fire, the dinner on the trail was often cooked in this manner. Hair of larger animals such as badgers, woodchucks, and squirrels, and the quills of porcupines were singed off, and then roasted. Eggs were boiled in a basket of water using hot rocks and often could be kept for several days to a few weeks.

The Maidu used many methods of catching fish. Fish were plentiful and provided great quantities of flesh food second only to deer. Trout caught in nets and basket traps were clubbed and gathered into large baskets. Men made wicker traps out of willow withes. Though the design varied, these traps were usually conical in shape. The mouth of the trap was constructed with loose willows ribs attached to the brim. These loose ends were directed inside toward the bottom of the cone. The fish would swim past this loose construction but were unable to retreat because of the obstruction caused by the loose ribs. The bottom of the cone was tied and could be opened when the fastening was removed to retrieve the fish. A bow-type of net which was as wide as a small stream was laid across the water and fish drifting with the current were easily captured. Narrow streams were sometimes dammed so that marooned fish in the channel below the dam could be scooped up in baskets. The Indians also used fiber lines and sharp bone hooks baited with grasshoppers to catch fish.[37]

Salmon were not known in Indian Creek so the Maidu of Indian Valley traveled to Salmon Falls on the North Fork of the Feather River near Big Meadows to get these fish when they were plentiful. [38]

The Maidu cooked fish by boiling them in baskets with hot rocks or roasted them on sticks over coals. If a great number of fish were caught, they were cleaned, heads and backbones removed and strung up unsalted on poles to dry. Dried fish were tied and stacked in bales or packed in large baskets for winter use. The women cooked the salmon in earth pit ovens, and then dried the meat on poles. When thoroughly dry it was crumbled and stored for later use.[39]

TOOLS and IMPLEMENTS

The grinding of food was an important task. Flat bedrocks near villages or harvesting sites served as grinding slabs for nuts and seeds. When the grinding area became deeply worn, the meal would pack in the bottom and then the grinding spot would be abandoned in favor of a new one. Large loose flat stones were used as well and since they were portable the women carried them to their dwellings and harvesting sites.

When a basket hopper was employed over a grinding slab, the stone pestle used was long and flat on the grinding end. The pestle was used in a vertical position. When the grinding slab was used without a hopper basket, the milling stone was oval or rectangular in shape. None of these stones had any ornamentation.

Portable globular mortars, thought to have been made by ancient tribes, were sought after but were feared. Families who had these in their possession kept them buried some distance from the dwelling only to be dug up for occasional inspection. The shaman used them for ceremonial purposes as it was believed that these mortars possessed supernatural powers. They also believed that the globular mortars were made by Coyote at the time of Creation and he scattered them about the earth for the use of man.[40] Other Maidu believed that the mortars were once people and looked upon them as hallowed items.[41]

Rocks used in cooking were chosen freely and usually were round in shape. Two sticks aided the handling of the hot rocks. Spoons were unknown. Knives were crudely chipped out of obsidian or chert and more often were without handles. Bone or wood handles were put on a few blades and tied with sinew. Bone awls or basket needles, *his kum bum mim*, were about six inches long and usually had wrapped handles. Soap-root fiber brushes, *hey yem*, aided the women in their manufacture of acorn flour.

Fire making was of great importance and, because it required great skill and effort, the fire burned continuously. Men made the fires by twirling a long wood rod made of buckeye one-half inch in diameter on a notched block of incense cedar. A tinder bed of shredded grass or cedar helped the spark grow into flame. Buck-eye fire-making sticks commanded quite a price. [42]

In hunting large game, the bow and arrow was the primary weapon. Bows were made out of yew wood which was traded from the Atsugewi to the north. The wood was selected, split, and shaved down to the right form and thickness with flint and pumice stone. In order to obtain the right shape with an incurve center and recurve tips, the piece of wood was wrapped in green grass and heated slowly in hot ashes. The wood was then bent to the required shape which it retained when cool. Short strips of sinew softened by chewing, were applied to the back of the bow with glue made from boiled salmon skins. These strips were rubbed with a flat bone to attain smoothness. Red and green geometric designs were painted on with a tip of a feather. Bowstrings were a two-ply cord of sinew which had been softened by chewing and twisted by rolling between the open palm and the thigh. Salmon glue was rubbed in during the twisting process to make the fibers stick together.

Arrows were flint-tipped and the shafts were made of cane or rose and had fore-shafts of serviceberry which were cut into a dowel on one end and then inserted into the pithy center of the main shaft. This joint was wrapped with sinew. The butt end was notched one-fourth of an inch and an obsidian tip was inserted, bound with sinew, and the union waterproofed with a pitch covering. Two grooved pumice stones were employed to straighten the shaft. The fore-shaft was painted red as an indication of poison and stripes of color on the nock indicated ownership. Feathers were split midrib and were applied to the shaft with pitch about a finger's width below the nock end. Three feathers about four inches long were applied, trimmed with a hot coal, and sinew wrapping held each end down. Feathers of hawks were usually used, but the finest arrows for large game, deer and bear, were eagle feathers. Arrow points were most frequently made of obsidian, dull black basalt lava, or chert of various colors. Arrows for large game were thirty inches long. Shorter untipped arrows of cane were used for small mammals and birds.

For shooting, bows were held either at a 45 degree angle or horizontally with the arrow on top. The primary release of the arrow was used. A skin of a small mammal, turned fur-side in, served as the quiver. A thong tied between the pair of forelegs and pair of hindlegs provided a comfortable shoulder strap for the hunter.[43]

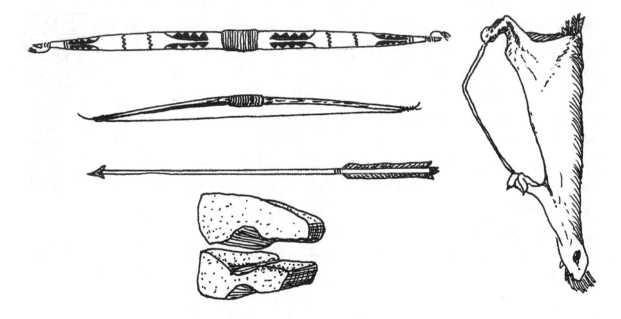

A.   (Top) Maidu bow forty inches long and two inches wide, deer sinew backed and painted with green powder traded from the Achomawi to the north. Powder was mixed with salmon glue. Arrow is obsidian tipped. (After Dixon).

B.   (Lower Left) Maidu arrow straightener and smoother of sandstone about three inches long. (After Dixon).

C.   (Right) Mountain Maidu arrow quiver made of a small animal skin turned inside-out. (After Schultz).

BASKETRY

Houses, tools, and clothing of the Maidu of Indian Valley proved that they were people living in the Stone Age, but along with many other tribes in California their basketry excelled that of any other tribes on the continent.[44] The basketry of the Northeastern Maidu was recognized as some of the best in California in craftsmanship and diversity of types surpassed only by the ornate quality of the Pomo.[45]

Baskets provided containers for the preparation and serving of food, storage, and transport. Each use demanded certain strength, size, and shape. In order to meet these demands, the Maidu women wove in the following characteristic styles: the coiled method, the twined method and wickerwork.

Techniques of coiled basketry required skill and patience as much time was demanded to produce a basket of quality. Three parallel rods of willow, maple or redbud provided the warp. This core ran as a continuous spiral with each row lashed into the top rod of the previous row by weft of redbud or maple. In order to accomplish this process, the weft was pushed apart between each two stitches with an awl thus making a hole large enough to slip a weft strand through. The weft strand was carried around the new core and put through the next awl hole (see Figures on pages 19 and 20). Most of the baskets were of the coiled type.

Twined basketry required warp of radiating willow ribs from a central point. These were lashed together by two (or four) weft strands, with each strand covering one side (in and out) of a warp rib (see Figure on page 19). Pine root was used as weft when setting up the radiating ribs, as it did not slip on the smooth willow. Bear grass was the main weft after the center had been established with the pine root. These baskets were tightly woven by placing a strand of pine root under each strand of bear grass. Twined baskets were made into burden baskets, hopper baskets and storage baskets. (see Figures on page 22).

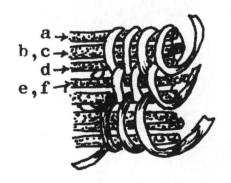
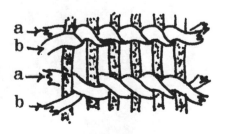

A. (Left) Technique of coiled basketry using three willow rods. (after Otis T. Mason). Note that lashing strand anchors three new rods *a, b,* and *c* to the top rib *d* of the preceding *d, e,* and *f* group.

B. (Right) Twined basketry employs two weft or lashing strands. With overlaying as when pine root is placed under bear grass, there will be two strands for *a* and two for *b*.

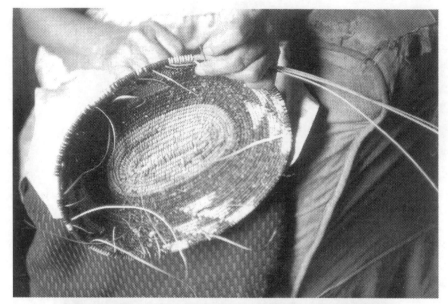

Daisy Baker demonstrates the technique of making a coiled basket using three willow rods for warp, redbud and maple for weft. Loose ends will be rubbed off when the basket is finished. In the lower picture, weft materials are in the foreground basket.

(Upper) Bottoms of three coiled baskets showing varied designs. The two smaller ones were made by Daisy Baker showing a wing design (left) and a bear eye design (right0. Lilly Baker made the basket with the butterfly design using split maple and fern root.

(Middle) Small coiled baskets used as drinking vessels. Designs are bear eye, *panom henim* (left), and bear paw, *panom bechee* (right). Both baskets were made by Daisy Baker.

(Lower) Large coiled plate or tray seventeen inches in diameter made by Daisy Baker using maple strips (background), redbud (red-brown design), and fern root (black design). The design is the bird wing, *yeh yum*.

(Upper) A small burden basket of simple design, redbud and bear grass, made by Daisy Baker. Note the pine root point. Pine root was used to start many baskets because it would not slip out of place when the weaver was beginning the basket.

(Lower) Twined baskets and bottle made by Daisy Baker. The creel and bottle are modern innovations in basketry. The basket on the left hangs on the wall and is made to store small objects.

(Upper) `Kate Meadows McKinney with a collection of baskets made by members of the Meadows and Baker families. Mrs. McKinney sits with baskets and beadwork showing her workmanship. She also made the basket on the table to the left with the eagle design.

(Lower) Daisy baker, Kate's daughter, made the two large plates on the ground to the left. Daisy's grandmother, Jenny Meadows, made the larger burden basket behind the eagle basket. This basket is over three feet in length. The collection of these baskets is presently at the Salem residence on Lake Almanor, California. (Copies of pictures taken in 1930)

Wicker baskets were woven entirely of willow loosely woven in a style similar to twining. Willow rods formed a weft which passed around two willow warp ribs instead of one, as in the twining. In the next row, these two ribs would be separated and paired with the neighboring ribs. Alternating these two rows, the women were able to construct sturdy beaters. Sieves and trays (see Figures on page 24).

(Upper) Beater or sieve, *lok som,* made from willow withes in
a wicker type of weave made by Daisy Baker.

(Lower) Three wicker sieves of different shapes. The one on the right is
dark with age and use. It was made by Kate McKinney. The center conical
shaped sieve, also made by Kate McKinney, was used to catch fish.

Before the weaving could commence, the women had to spend much time gathering and preparing materials. Young girls were patiently taught skills of preparation by old women. Much practice was required to develop knowledge of material selection, adeptness in preparation, and weaving. Weaving continued throughout the year as baskets were very important to the existence of the Maidu.

Gathering of most materials was seasonal. If picked or gathered prematurely or past prime, the materials were difficult to handle for numerous reasons. The flow of sap in the woody materials possibly affected quality, as spring and late fall were chosen to collect willow, maple and redbud withes. The bark "slipped" easily off those collected in the spring and had to be scraped in the fall.

Willow, *pom*, was the most abundant material. This grey-leaf willow (*Salix argyrophlla*) provided the white cane when peeled of its bark. *Hee be*, commonly called deer brush, was sturdier than willow and also light in color. When the bark was removed the weaver carefully scraped each stem with a sharp piece of obsidian down to a uniform size (see Figure on page 25). Willow, deer brush, and bitter cherry were used as foundation material in all techniques of weaving. One rod of bitter cherry, *see lay wa*, with two rods of willow made a very firm coiled basket.

Lilly and Kit are taking the willow leaves off while Daisy scrapes and peels the bark off leaving clear white willow withes.

Maple, *dap pe*, required more preparation, and shrubs were not as numerous. The Maidu "cultivated" both willow and maple in Indian Valley by either burning or cutting back clumps so that long straight shoots would come forth. These were harvested in a year or two.[46] Maple stalks were larger than willow, sometimes one-half inch in diameter. These were heated slowly in hot ashes and when evenly brown they were split three ways. After an incision was made in the large end, one section was held with the teeth while the other two sections were pulled away carefully with the hands trying to maintain uniformity in each piece. The bark separated easily from the stalk leaving a shiny neutral surface. The pithy heart was removed and each piece could be split several times then scraped to the desired size.[57]

Redbud, *lil lee*, grew in the foothills. The bark provided design material on coiled and twined baskets and was important enough for the Indians to travel on snowshoes in the spring to lower elevations to collect it. The material was gathered and processed on the spot if time allowed. Then the withes were tied in bundles and carried home on their backs with a buckskin thong around the shoulders or on the forehead to hold the bundle in place.[48]

Bear grass, *che ta com,* could be gathered only during two weeks in mid-July. New central leaves plucked from the clump and processed further by removing the mid-rib when dry provided the chief overlay in twined basketry.[49]

The root of the ponderosa pine, *ba bom cha,* required digging. Sometimes the high water of spring floods exposed roots along banks and those fortunate enough to find these were relieved of the long tedious process of digging. Only strong flexible roots met the standards and these were cut off with a small obsidian knife or burned off slowly with a fire. The women chose lengths of root about four feet long and roasted these slowly in hot ashes. Becoming soft and pliable, the roots could be split, first in quarters, then into half inch strips. Dixon states that these Indians sometimes dyed the pine root black by burying it in mud mixed with charcoal.

Maidenhair fern stems were collected in August.[50] Fern, *so la lum,* provided most of the black in designs. Maidenhair did not grow in Indian Valley and possibly collected on trips to the north. The common bracken fern did grow in the valley, and the Indians used the two inner layers of these roots whenever possible.

As soon as materials were collected, weaving commenced. Materials in preparation for weaving were soaked in a watertight basket. An awl, *his kum bum mim,* and a small glass scraper, *cham me,* were two important tools. The weaver placed in the water only the materials she could use within a certain period of time, as oversaturation was carefully avoided. As the basket progressed in size, it was liberally moistened. When finished and dry, loose ends were rubbed off.[51]

With utility in mind, the weaver developed the shape carefully. Each shape had a purpose (see Figure on page 24). Coiled baskets for food or storage varied in size, a few inches to three feet in diameter. These baskets were woven so tightly that they held water and provided excellent storage.

Designs varied and were inspired by familiar motifs: mountains, clouds, bushes, vines, butterflies, earthworms, quail tips, rattlesnakes, duck wings, eyes, fish teeth, and arrow points. Usually only one symbol was developed on a basket with variations of the same motif. When a person worked full time, an average basket was produced in two weeks. Beaters of wickerwork were made in several hours (see Figures on page 24).

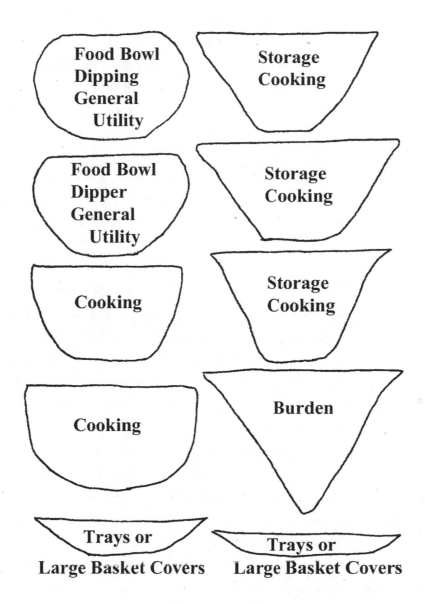

Basic Coiled Shapes   **Basic Twined Shapes**

TANNING

Maidu men employed several methods when tanning hides. They buried bear skins and even used ashes to help dehair them. Deer hides were soaked thoroughly for several days, then scraped with a bone scraper to dehair them and remove excess flesh. The tanning agent was a mixture of deer brains, cooked, mashed, mixed with dried moss, and then molded into small cakes for storage. The agent was rubbed and worked into the scraped hide. The hide was then soaked overnight in a solution containing the agent. While drying in the sun the next day, the hide was stretched and worked by hand to make it pliable and soft.[52]

Skin blankets were woven of one-inch strips of rabbit fur. These were not tanned, so when they dried they curled and twisted with the fur side out. By tying ends of strips together, a long fur-covered rope was formed. This was wrapped around upright roles to form a double warp. The weft of the same material was woven through the horizontal warp and produced a very soft, fluffy, and warm blanket. [55]

Skins of other animals were cured in the method described for deer. Should eventual use demand it, some skins were not tanned at all and used as rawhide. It was used on the bottom of hopper baskets for edging, snowshoes, the base of baby baskets, and whole skins for bow quivers.

TRANSPORTATION, TRAILS, and TRADE

Travel was by foot or by water, as the horse was unknown to these Indians before the arrival of the pioneers. The Northeastern Maidu may have seen horses on journeys to the north or east, as their eastern neighbors of the Great Basin area had been introduced to the advantages of speedier transportation via horseback many years before.[54]

Indian Valley carried the overflow of spring floods. Pools and marshes remained throughout the year in a large area of the valley floor. Blunt-ended dug-out canoes were constructed out of pine or cedar logs. These logs were usually windfalls and hollowed out by controlled burning. Two to four persons could ride in these crude affairs by propelling themselves with a pole or a single-bladed paddle about three feet long. However, rafts of three or four logs tied together, the usual mode of water transportation, were propelled by a pole.

Trails in Indian Valley were well worn to favorite harvesting spots and hunting areas. Trails followed canyon bottoms and went over mountain saddles to each neighboring valley. Bruff in his wanderings of 1850 followed numerous Indian trails, and it was probable that an Indian trail eventually brought him and his party into Indian Valley. The trail over Grizzly Range to American Valley to the southeast was later converted into a wagon road by early pioneers. Mountain Meadows was accessible by trail up Cook's Canyon. The trail to Big Meadows followed Haun's Creek, a tributary to Wolf Creek.

These people traded with their neighbors, especially with those in the north, the Atsugewi and Achomawi. They also traded with the Northwestern Maidu, Washo, and Northern Paiute. The Maidu received from the Atsugewi bows, twined baskets, horses, and furs in exchange for deer hides, clam disc beads, and coiled baskets. The Achomawi gave them obsidian, green pigment, shell beads, bows, arrows, and skins for clam disc beads, salt and digger pine nuts. These last three items were undoubtedly obtained from the hill or Northwestern Maidu, as they were items the hill people traded for bows and arrows, skins, sugar pine nuts, acorns, deer hides, and miscellaneous foods.[55] The Maidu of Indian Valley refused to allow much trade with eastern neighbors, as some hostility did exist over the Paiutes and Washo coming into the valley to steal women for wives.[56] Kroeber, however, reports that wild tobacco from the Honey Lake region was traded in all directions.[57]

SOCIAL PRACTICES

Marriage among the mountain Maidu was often arranged by the parents with an exchange of several strings of clam-shell beads as a small payment. Mates were always chosen from another village. Sometimes a family feast marked the occasion; otherwise ceremonies were non-existent and the boy and girl just began living together. They lived first with the girl's family, and after a period of time they moved to the husband's village. Having two wives was common practice and only men of great wealth had more. When the wife died the husband was obligated to marry her sister, and when the husband died, his brother married the widow. Mothers-in-law could not look at their sons-in-law.

Infrequently divorces did occur. When children were involved, the mother took the girls and the boys stayed with the father. Separation took place for the following reasons: the husband mistreated his wife; the husband failed to provide food and clothing for the family; or the wife was lazy and barren. When the wife was returned to her family for the last reason, the payment was returned or they sent an ex-sister-in-law to the husband for an additional sum.[58]

After the birth of a child, the mother remained in isolation and restrictions were placed upon both the mother and father... Eating dried or fresh meat was forbidden for a certain period of time. It was wished that the umbilical cord would be shed as soon as possible, as it was this event which relieved the couple of the post-birth taboos. The father could not smoke or gamble. Sweating or bathing released them from the taboos.[59]

Cradle baskets were made in two shapes. A small one without a hood was used first. This was made of willow ribs laid in parallel rows on an oval frame of service berry or oak. The ribs were bound on to the frame with leather thongs. As the baby grew, a larger cradle was made. It had a willow rib hood and the frame was a vee shape so that the bottom could be stuck in the ground while the mother was at work. The baby was wrapped in buckskin and lashed to the frame. Another skin or large leaves were used as a diaper. The mother carried the frame on her back with a thong band across the shoulders or forehead. The baby outgrew about three cradles before he was allowed to crawl or walk. The mother often nursed the child until he was two or three years old. As children grew up, grandmothers often assumed the responsibility for their care while mothers concentrated efforts toward the gathering and preparing of food.

Twins were feared and the Maidu thought they were bad luck. It was thought that if the father wore two caps, *wika,* at the time of conception, twins would be the result. Infanticide was sometimes practiced when the mother died in childbirth.[60]

Extensive ceremonies were performed as puberty rites for each girl as she attained womanhood. These gatherings enabled the girl's family to look over prospective mates for the daughter. People were summoned from a distance by smoke signals lit in the hills by girl and her mother. The girl carried a deer-hoof rattle for ten days during which men and women danced. Taboos were enforced upon the girl. She fasted two or three days in seclusion and carried wood for the fires each morning and evening as though preparing herself for future life. Her ears were pierced by her mother with a wooden awl. On the last night, only the women and girls danced. The ceremony concluded at noon and the girls bathed in a nearby stream, then raced back to the house. The remainder of the day was spent in feasting and playing games.[61]

In the late spring, the Bear Dance was performed. The bear was a symbol of evil and stood for all that the Maidu feared. The rattlesnake was the second thing feared most. People came together for the dance, which lasted three days, to the abode of a shaman, who was annually responsible for the rites. It was noisy and feasting, dancing, and singing was enjoyed. Men and women danced in separate rings. Sometimes men wearing bearskin robes participated in ceremonies and a bear hide would be hung high in a tree or on a pole to be "chased away." A long and slender piece of maple bark, symbolizing the rattlesnake, was hung up on a maple pole. After the ceremonies of dancing and singing, the people returned to their homes feeling cleansed of all evil and were ready to go out and safely gather food and materials for the year.[62]

For various ceremonies, the shaman wore a headband of stiff quill feathers from the red-shafted flicker. The Indians also made belts on which the showy greenish feathered neck skins of the male mallard duck were attached. During ceremonies, small tufts of feathers would be tucked into the hair.[63]

Upon death the body was placed in a flexed position and wrapped in a hide for burial. Once in a while the mountain people placed the body in a basket before wrapping it in a hide. All property of the deceased was broken and placed in the grave with the addition of a basket of water. This water carried the deceased on the long journey ahead. Wailing by the mourners and the family lasted for days. Taboos were enforced for all mourners and the family. For four or five days no meat was eaten. Widows cut their hair closely and covered their heads with pitch and charcoal. It was left on until it wore off of its own accord. Restrictions were not so severe or lengthy for widowers.

The annual mourning ceremony, sometimes called "burning" or "cry", was held in the autumn on a hill near a cemetery site. Wailing took place as possessions, sacrifices to honor the dead, were placed on poles within the burning enclosure. At a certain time during the ceremony, a shaman lit the fires to burn all things within the enclosure. The tempo of the wailing increased as the fires burned baskets, bows, robes, and other objects which probably took months to make.

Generally speaking, the Indians of Indian Valley were happy and jovial. Both men and women enjoyed story telling, games, and gambling. Sweating was formalized in the large sweat house with shaman conducting. Musical instruments, the flute and bow, were played for pleasure or in courtship. Ball games were played with a double-ended hide ball and proceeded like shinny. Women hit the ball with a stick in their game and the men kicked it.

STORIES OF CREATION and BELIEFS

Creation myths of the Northeastern Maidu of Indian Valley did not give any suggestion that they had knowledge of any other region, thereby suggesting migration. The story was told: The Creation was a beginning, before which there was nothing. *Kodoyanpe,* the Earthmaker or Creator, and Coyote were floating many days in a canoe on a great sea. They saw an object like a bird's nest floating on the surface to which *Kodoyanpe* fastened ropes in five directions, East, South West, Northwest, and North. Coyote's evil came forth in a song, the burden of which was that the earth should be made rugged and difficult for traveling. *Kodoyanpe* told Coyote to lie flat on his face, and proceeded to stretch the tiny mass so that no one could see the end of it. Coyote left to inspect the earth and *Kodoyanpe* set out on his own tour. At all places he left pairs of men as tiny as seed and planted each under a gopher hill. He gave each pair a name and a country; thus he made as many pairs as there are tribes and people. He returned and built his house and soon Coyote came back and built his house, too (Earthmaker's stone canoe is visible today on top of Keddie Peak, north of Indian Valley.)

A period of conflict began; all caused by Coyote, so *Kodoyanpe* called a council of all people and asked them to destroy Coyote. They killed all coyotes except one, and they tried numerous ways to kill him, but he always escaped. Angered, Earthmaker took all of his possessions, headed east and left the world. Then the human pairs came to life to begin existence in the world of labor, pain, and death all made by Coyote.[647]

Coyote became the main character in many a tale. Typical of most tales was the story of "Coyote and the Fleas:"

> The Coyote was walking along the road one day, and came to where a Mole was working. He stood and watched the Mole for a while, and then stuck his foot down in front of the Mole, and kicked him out of the ground, saying, "Hello, Cousin," The Mole had a little sack that he was carrying, and the Coyote, thinking that it contained tobacco, said, "Here, give me a smoke." The Mole replied, "No, I have no tobacco." The Coyote answered, "Why, yes, you have some in that little sack." The Mole repeated that he had no tobacco, that there was none in the sack. "Let me look

in the sack," said Coyote. "No, you can't look at it," said the Mole. "Well, then, if you won't let me, I will take it away from you," and the Coyote grabbed the sack, and took it away. He opened it, and found that it was full of fleas. They jumped all over him, and began to bite him. The Coyote cried, "Take it back, Cousin, take it back," but the Mole had run to his hole and disappeared. The Coyote was left to howl alone. After a while he looked around, and said, "People can call me Coyote." [65]

Roland B. Dixon collected many similar stories as part of the work of the C. P. Huntington Expedition during the summer of 1899 among the *Koyama,* or Maidu of the high Sierra in the vicinity of Genesee and Taylorsville. In all such stories the Coyote acts as a marplot to the plans of *Kodoyanpe,* the Creator.

Tales varied from village to village. Keddie Ridge is the location of several often-told myths:

The Indian on the ridge is sleeping. He had been sent all over the world to measure the waters in all the lakes and oceans. When he got to Homer Lake, near the top of Keddie Ridge, he put his measuring stick in the lake. He was so tired, he decided to lie down to rest. He did so, and went to sleep. He has never awakened.

January is the month when, according to the Indians, the blasted tree in Homer Lake, at the base of Mt. Keddie, turns once around. The great water spirit, imprisoned in its base, raises its head to take its yearly look at the world. Woe to the mortals who are unfortunate enough to be seen by him, for he fascinates and draws them down into his abode and devours them. This is the water spirit that had caused the people no end of trouble when they arrived in a great canoe at the lake which is presently Indian Valley. The water finally found an outlet and drained out to the ocean and the valley was dry land. This water spirit caused the people so much trouble that by command of the Great Chief the spirit was imprisoned in Homer Lake to remain there until the end of time.

After a series of visions and dreams, a medicine man went up Keddie Ridge to Homer Lake. He went down the petrified tree in the center of the lake and came up at Big Springs in Big Meadows.[66]

The Maidu told stories to each other only in the winter. They felt that if a story was told in the spring, summer, or fall the greatly feared rattlesnake would come from his den and listen, bringing bad luck. It was thought that telling stories about water snakes and frogs would bring rain. Further, stories told out of season made a very cold and snowy summer,[67] and if told in the daytime the narrator would become crooked or blind.

Five was the only sacred number, and among the mountain people there were five points to the compass: of west, northwest, north, east and south.

These natives believed that spirits inhabited the whole countryside, under the earth, and in the sky. The spirits were associated with prominent rocky peaks, cliffs, waterfalls, and lonely mountain lakes. Every shaman had one or more of these spirits for his guardians, and they aided him in whatever he did.

In order to have insight on the future, the Maidu looked to the moon. If the first quarter of the moon stood with the points of the crescent upwards, it denoted a season of fruit, good weather, and freedom from sickness. Should the moon appear with its points directed horizontally, it denoted a poor season, bad weather and sickness. Additional concepts of the heavens were that they thought stars were made of something soft like buckskin and thunder was a boy who ate trees.

When a child's teeth came loose and dropped out, the Maidu would guarantee strong teeth for the child by immediately putting the tooth down a gopher hole.

The root of a certain plant was rubbed on the legs to keep rattlesnakes away. If this same root were chewed, one could blind a rattlesnake by spitting at him. It thundered at once when a person was bitten by a rattlesnake. Thunder also occurred when a great man died, or when a woman had a miscarriage.[68]

All of these traditions, customs, and habits were well ingrained in the lives of the Northeastern Maidu of Indian Valley. Discovery of gold brought into the area foreigners, who, with new ideas and conflicting traditions, disregarded these easy-going people and their rights as humans. For two decades following 1851, the Maidu were forced to move and concentrate their numbers while the white men took over the land and indoctrinated these Indians in the "civilized" way of life.

Chapter III
FIRST WHITE SETTLERS and SETTLEMENT of INDIAN VALLEY

The rugged country and inaccessibility of this region discouraged exploration by early trail blazers and mountain men; in fact, the whole of Plumas County remained unsettled by white men before 1850. Thousands of miners, fired by Stoddard's story of a mythical gold lake, crisscrossed the northern Sierra in a vain search. However, it took discovery of gold to draw white settlers to these mountains. Even after gold had been discovered here, immigrant gold seekers felt that they must reach Sacramento. These inexperienced miners passed mining camp after mining camp to reach Sacramento Valley, only to discover that they had to retrace their steps to a camp they had passed a few weeks before.[1]

Peter Lassen, the old scout who had opened an immigrant road in 1848, was restless on his ranch near Red Bluff and began taking short cuts into the mountains prospecting, but with little success. Stoddard's story stirred Lassen's prospecting fever and he organized a party which consisted of a large company of men, Indians with their squaws, beef cattle, pack horses, and mules. They left Lassen's Rancho on July 14, 1850, and were followed a few days later by Bruff with five friends, pack animals, and supplies.[2] As was their intention, Bruff's party soon joined Lassen's and they spent the next three months wandering through the mountains looking for the mythical lake. These seekers of gold religiously followed Indian trails and finally explored territory previously not known to white men.

Bruff reported in his journal that they spent the night in Indian Valley on October 12, 1850, after spending many days traveling in a westerly direction from Lake Derby, Bruff's name for Honey Lake. While in Indian Valley, Bruff observed that the trail had been " … much traveled by adventurers as ourselves. The prospectors call this stream the N. branch of the Middle Fork of the Feather river." He added that he recognized the valley as a place they had visited earlier and where he had discovered a vein of gold-bearing quartz.[3]

Two days later "Old Pete" expressed unwillingness to return to the settlements and confided that he wished to return to Indian Valley and pass the winter. Ten others resolved to winter in the mountains with Lassen and immediately made an estimate of supplies needed for the next six months.[4]

Lassen remained in the mountains with several companions and the others returned to the settlements to get supplies. They discovered that it was impossible to find the number of pack animals Lassen wanted, as other prospecting parties had depleted the supply. Campbell and Meyerwitz decided to return to the mountains with enough supplies to bring the others in.

Despite the lack of pack animals, Lassen was determined to winter in the mountains; hence he soon returned to the settlements with Hough Sr. to get supplies. Lassen related that when they left the Feather River valley, they had tried to persuade a couple of Indian boys to accompany them as Lassen was eager to show these "children of the mountains the settlements and then return them home. The boys agreed and even hopped into the wagon, but soon adult Indians overtook them and refused to let the boys go.

After gathering the necessary provisions, Lassen and his comrades fitted a couple of wagons which were to carry supplies as far as possible. Since the men all had mounts, they planned to use the oxen for meat after they had served as pack animals. On November 15, Lassen, Burton, Isadore, Jones, Hough Sr., Campbell and two others moved off to winter in the mountains.[5]

It was probable that Lassen and his companions did winter that year in Indian Valley, as in 1851 Lassen and Burton had the only white settlement in the valley, a square brush-covered cabin.[6] They opened a trading post, had the first garden, and raised turnips, beets, lettuce, and other vegetables. These rare products brought high prices from prospecting parties passing through the valley. Business was good and Lassen bestowed the name "Cache" upon the valley. However, because of the large number of Indians seen by travelers when they entered the valley, the name eventually became Indian Valley.[7]

Among the many groups of prospectors entering the valley in 1851 were John J.L. Peel, Wheeler, and Ryan. They had followed well-used Indian trails to track down a lead that there were rich diggings northeast of Indian Valley. Coming from American Valley, they crossed the mountain and camped north of where Taylorsville now stands. They headed northwest the next day and after passing *ko sim*, the large mound, they had to cross Lights Creek. An Indian camp stood across the river and a dugout was tied along the bank. The prospectors yelled at the Indians that they wanted to be ferried across. One Indian with some knowledge of English called back, "Five dollars." Wheeler had a temper and whipped out his revolver. He demanded that they bring the canoe over and Peel paid them a dollar for the trip. Peel confessed later that after seeing hundreds of Indians around him, he felt most uneasy until they returned the next day and were across the river again.

After prospecting briefly and seeing the dwelling Lassen had built in 1850, Peel and his companions returned to Nelson Creek. They extolled the beauties and promise of the valley to Taylor and his friends. Peel felt that as a result of this trip, he had influenced Jobe Taylor to settle in Indian Valley.[8] But Jobe Taylor had passed near Indian Valley as he had camped at Big Meadows, seven miles away, on October 31 in 1849 when he followed the Lassen Trail with hundreds of other migrants headed for Sacramento.[9]

In 1852, Jobe Taylor and Warren Meeker came from Nelson Point to Indian Valley in February and put up notice claiming the land now occupied by Taylorsville. In March, Peter Lassen, Isadore Meyerwitz, and George St. Felix arrived to open their trading post. They replaced the brush with a permanent roof and started the garden with a greater variety of vegetables. By the summer Taylor had built a house on his claim and in the fall a number of settlers had chosen locations and built cabins. Many emigrants had come through the valley from the east through Beckwourth Pass.

Everyone purchased potatoes, turnips, cabbages, beets, and lettuce from Lassen at the regular price of fifteen cents per pound. Taylor and his friends helped harvest the crops and sack vegetables. An emigrant once sent his little girl to Mr. Taylor for turnips and Taylor related, "She gave me ten cents, and I told her to go to the sack and help herself. She took one that weighed eight pounds, which cost us $1.20."

A voting precinct was established that fall at Taylor's house, so that the settlers could participate in the presidential election. In August, Mrs. Dr. Cory gave birth to a daughter, the first white child to be born in the valley.[10]

The winter of 1852-3 was one not to be forgotten by these pioneers. In November heavy snows blocked mountain trails and late shipments expected by merchants never arrived. Those without a secure supply of stores held out in mining camps as long as they dared and then panicked to the nearest mountain settlement only to discover low supplies there. Many miners struggled to get through the deep snows to the lower settlements; some succeeded and others perished along the way. The experiences of this winter proved that life in the mountains should be planned with future needs in mind.

That spring Taylor and Meeker built a frame barn, the first in the county. They also put in a crop of wheat and barley. The emigration was large and the valley became settled, with large parcels of land set aside for cultivation. Ledges of quartz-bearing gold attracted miners to establish claims in the mountains surrounding the valley and small mining camps appeared overnight, only to vanish when the ledges played out.

Taylor, an experienced surveyor, took it upon himself to subdivide the town of Taylorsville. As the largest settlement of the valley, it continued to grow as an agricultural community. His place was used as a hotel and place of entertainment and the town gradually grew around it. Taylor built a sawmill in 1855 and a grist mill in 1856.[11] The grist mill stones were shipped to California on a sailing vessel which came around the Horn. Both the sawmill and grist mill were operated by the same water from a mill race built by Taylor (see Figure on page 47).

The sawmill was operated by one man. Logs on a track were pulled into the mill by a water-powered winch. A water-powered whip-like saw worked in an up-and-down motion and once it was going, the operator ran around to the other side and took the board off as it was cut. The process was repeated for each board. After piling the boards, the operator cut the edges off by going through the same process again.

Boards from the sawmill were used to build the three-story grist mill which was run by a man named Hough with the assistance of an Indian, Charlie Shunam.[12] Water diverted at a bulkhead came from the mill race to the basement of the mill to power the grinding stones. After the grain was ground, it was elevated on a wooden cleat belt to the top story, sifted through silk screen on the way down to the first floor where it was sacked. The grain came from the ranches in the valley and the flour supplied the local needs. After the mines in Idaho opened and trade between California and the new mining region started, surplus flour was shipped to Idaho and points beyond by pack train.[13]

GOVERNMENT INDIAN POLICY

The white settlers gradually claimed large areas of Indian Valley for farms. Soon the Indians here, as elsewhere in California, found themselves trespassers on lands where their ancestors lived for centuries. In 1850 the United States government began to recognize that some compensation should be made the California Indians for dispossessing them from their land, if only out of consideration for the safety of the intruding settlers. In 1851-2, five reservations were set up in the southern half of the state with most of $250,000 spent on one group of 700 Indians. Later Col. Thomas J. Henley added three more reservations: the Nome Lacke at Stony Creek, Round Valley in Mendocino, and Hoopa in the Klamath region. By 1857, over $12,000,000 had been spent by the federal government supposedly for the California Indians, but the mountain Indians were completely ignored in any of those efforts made by the federal government.[14]

The law which affected the Indian Valley Indians was passed by the California State Legislature on April 22, 1850. It was a special law which controlled their dim future and produced a traumatic change in the lives of many of the Indians of California:

> … confirmed them in possession of their villages, although owners white of the land were at liberty to arrange with them for occupancy some special sections of it. A confined tenancy at most, for neither land rights nor citizenship privileges was accorded. They might be hired to work under contract, and by special provision this was made to some extent compulsory by enabling local authorities to arrest all whom they chose to denominate as vagabonds and beggars, and turn them over to the highest

bidder for not exceeding four months. Any surplus wages after providing the victim clothes, was assigned to a mysterious Indian fund, unless relatives claimed the money. In cases of crime, juries might be demanded by either race, but white men could not convicted on Indian testimony … It was easy to charge anyone with vagabondage, especially by enlisting the potent aid of liquor, and obtain condemnation to forced labor. The impressments generally occurred toward harvest time, and this over, the poor wretches were sent adrift to starve, for their own harvest season was by this time lost to them.[15]

Indians were forbidden all firearms or liquor. Fences and "No trespassing" signs stopped mass drives for game. Many of the miners and settlers treated persons with Indian blood as slightly less than human, but on the other hand there were those who made efforts to live peacefully with the Indians.

PEACEFUL RELATIONS

By 1853, the natives of Indian Valley were finding acculturation in the white settler's way of life difficult, but generally they accepted the day-to-day experiences of being pushed about and off their land with calm submission. Many of the miners, ranchers and business men hired Indians to work for them. The general rule was that the Indian was treated kindly and the standard of $1.00 a day prevailed for years to come. Indians possessed one Indian name, but after working for a white employer for several years, he assumed the name of that employer. Some of these names were Forman, Boyden, Peter, Hedrick, Hamilton, and Taylor.

There were times when the Indian tried to work for the whites and they did not find jobs open to them. In order to live they had to steal stock, accept charity, or beg for food. In October, two Indians stole a horse belonging to A.C. Light. The thieves were captured and incarcerated in the barroom at Jobe Taylor's ranch. After tying their arms, Light guarded them but had to leave to go out to get wood for the fire. During his absence, the prisoners untied each other with their teeth and made an escape. One managed to get away, but the other was fatally shot by Taylor. The settlers buried him but the Indians found this disturbing, as they had not adopted the "civilized" plan of burial.

Jobe Taylor and others realized the necessity of creating goodwill among the natives in and around the valley. In November, a meeting was held by both the settlers and Indians in an attempt to reach some amicable plan of adjusting difficulties. Main participants of this powwow included Jobe Taylor, R.D. Smith, W.T. Ward, A.J. Ford, Chief Cheebeelicum, and an Indian boy, who was the interpreter. It was disclosed during the conference that the Indian Valley tribes had suffered from periodic incursions from the Pit River, Mill Creek, and Hat Creek tribes. The group decided that the rights and wrongs of each class should be considered in common, and that equal justice should be meted out when any wrong was done.[16]

This meeting reflected the spirit of Governor Peter Burnett's Annual Message, January 7, 1851, when speaking of his policy regarding the Indians:

> … considering the number and mere predatory character of the attacks at so many points along the whole frontier, I had determined in my own mind to leave the people of each neighborhood to protect themselves, believing they would be able to do so.[17]

The agreement between the white settlers and the Maidu was soon put to a test. In December George Rose, a blacksmith, entered Taylor's house for a drink Taylor was tending bar and an old Indian sat near the stove. When Rose saw the Indian, he shouted, "What business has that d——d Indian in this house." Taylor explained that he was a good Indian and only wanted to get warm. Rose walked up to the Indian and killed him. He then walked out, mounted his horse and rode off. A posse was organized and they found Rose barricaded in his shop, three miles below Taylor's. After parlaying some time, he agreed to let Fayette Gibson into the cabin. In a few moments Gibson managed to get the drop on Rose and turned him over to the posse for trial. The trial was held before a jury and W.T Ward acted as judge. The defendant was found guilty and executed two days after the shooting.

In January, a son of a North Arm chief, Rattlesnake, stole food and blankets from the cabin of Isaac hall and Howard Vandegriff, at the Hall ranch. He was pursued and captured. A jury of six men tried him at the house of W.T. Ward. They found him guilty and hung him between the Hall and Ward ranches on the north side of the valley. A number of Indian witnessed the execution without comment.[18]

Law that existed was found only in these self-constituted courts of miners and ranchers. There were no elected or appointed officials residing in Indian Valley; even getting married was a problem. In the spring of 1853, without minister or magistrate, Robert Ross and Mrs. Catherine Deitch solemnly declared themselves man and wife before witnesses. When they moved to Rush Creek that year, they were informed that their marriage was illegal and were married again by John Buckbee, a lawyer and miner. Later, when living in Onion Valley, a perambulating justice married them for the third time.[19]

The area now known as Plumas County, including IndianValley, constituted a part of Butte County. As the population rapidly increased, it became evident that if the mountain people were to have protection of law, schools, and roads, they should have their own county government close at hand in the mountains. The people of the eastern part of Butte County supported this separation of the county. On March 18, 1854, Plumas County was formed out of a northeastern portion of Butte County, including a large portion of the future Lassen County.

The people of Plumas County were authorized to hold a county election the second Saturday of April, 1854, to elect a judge, district attorney, clerk, sheriff, surveyor, assessor, coroner, and treasurer. From Indian Valley, experienced W. T. Ward was elected County

Judge and Jobe Taylor as County Surveyor. Indicative of the times was the decision of the tie vote between John R. Buckbee and his opponent, Christopher Porter, for County Assessor. Friends of Porter challenged Buckbee to play a game of seven-up for the office. The play-off was held at the Bradley Hotel in American Valley amidst a crowd of spectators. Buckbee arose from the table the winner of the game and office.[20]

In 1854 the larger settlements of Plumas County were situated in the Sierra, American, Indian, and Honey Lake Valleys. Travelers found the mountain trails connecting these valleys impassable for three to five months in the winter. Erratic communication existed and those living in the valleys other than American Valley, the county seat, paid little attention to their responsibilities as county residents for the next few years. Though Indian Valley was fairly close to American Valley, many travelers from the east followed a main trail or wagon road into Indian Valley from Beckwourth Pass following Red Clover and Indian Creeks bypassing Quincy. Many travelers and prospectors came over this road and continued northeast to Honey Lake Valley. William H. Nobles had done this in 1851, and had gone on to discover Nobles Road and Pass, later, frequently shortened to "Noble". It was claimed that Peter Lassen had been his guide.[21] The settlers and Indians of Indian Valley carried on friendly intercourse with the Honey Lake settlers and Indians. While residing in Indian Valley, Lassen prospected in the mountains between the two valleys. In 1855, he and Meyerwitz moved from Indian Valley and settled near Honey Lake.[22]

When Plumas County became established as a bona fide California county, some settlers of Honey Lake disclaimed being a part of said county and state. Others believed that Honey Lake was a part of California and Plumas County and owned taxable property elsewhere in the county. Taxes had to be paid in person at the Sheriff's Office in Quincy on the third Monday in October. Those in outlying districts found it difficult to get to Quincy to pay their taxes. The lengthy list of delinquent taxpayers in 1858, including thirty-nine names from Indian Valley and twice the number from Honey Lake, proved that the new county had problems.[23]

Indian trouble occurred frequently in the Honey Lake area and more than once the residents of Indian Valley became deeply involved in skirmishes and forays. Peaceful Indian Valley Indians, "Old Tom" and "Old Charley" and their families, lived many years in the upper part of Honey Lake Valley and the settlers had made peace with the local Paiutes through Chief Winnemuca. Harassment came from the northern Paiutes, Pit Rivers (Achomawis), Hat Creeks (Atsugewis), in the northwest, and from the Washo in the south.[24]

INDIAN TROUBLES

The infamous Potato War of Honey Lake in October, 1857, brought Indian Valley settlers and Indians to the aid of their neighbors. The Washo stole all of the potatoes from the William Morehead ranch while Morehead was away. When he returned and discovered the theft, he alerted his neighbors and they took out after the Indians and killed three. Later they made a dash upon the Indian camp and retrieved some potatoes but killed no Indians. Joe Eppstein, meanwhile, had gone to Indian Valley and returned with ten men and supplies. After thirty-five to forty men gathered, they decided to attack the Indians on the Crawford and Fullbright place on October 17th. During this skirmish, seven to eleven Indians were killed, fourteen wounded and only Eppstein was wounded among the whites. The whites entrenched themselves and it was reported that the Indians attacked on the 18th, but later this proved to be a false report.

Meanwhile, J. Williams of Honey Lake and M Milleston of Indian Valley started for Sacramento with a petition asking Governor Johnson for military aid. The petition stated that all of the Indian tribes, numbering in the thousands, had commenced hostilities against the whites with the intention of exterminating the whole white population of the area. Mr. Williams was reminded of the fact that the Honey Lakers disclaimed California and Plumas County, but Williams assured the governor that the citizens of Honey Lake were willing to come under jurisdiction of California were it proven they were within its boundaries. Williams also laid the case before Col. Thomas J. Henley, Superintendent of Indian Affairs, who sent a quantity of Indian goods to Lassen. As an Indian Agent, Lassen was expected to settle all difficulties without further bloodshed. General Kibbe sent sixty stands of arms, the Rangers hurried to the Fullbright and Crawford place and found no Indians to fight. Presumably, after making a treaty with Lassen, the Washo withdrew from the valley, never to return.[25]

Unfortunately, Indian troubles were not over for the Honey Lakers for some time to come, but the residents of Indian Valley were to experience only a few scares of consequence.

Around the time of the Potato War, J.J.L. Peel was working in Quincy when word arrived about an Indian scare in Indian Valley. An Indian wash-woman revealed to her mistress that the Indian Valley natives had induced the ones from Honey Lake to join them and drive all of the cattle and horses from Indian Valley, massacre the whites, and burn their houses. All of the Indians, about one thousand, with their possessions had disappeared from Indian Valley a week or two before. Peel and some of his friends gathered all the loose guns, a motley assortment, that they could find in Quincy and hurried to Indian Valley. A fort, or block house, had been built on the Israel Scott ranch, near Ward's ranch, and in Peel's appraisal it looked like a well-prepared invitation to be massacred. The men who built it had no concept of Indian warfare, and built it below the crest of a hill. After waiting for several days for an attack, it turned out that the Indians were "worse scared" than the whites and had left the valley because they heard that the whites were mobilizing against them.[26] A writer for the Plumas Argus, at that time, expressed an opinion by wondering why these savages were not on reservations.[27]

In the winter of 1858, Uriah (Ry) and James Shaffer of North Arm discovered that they had been robbed of a calf and wheat, flour, and potatoes from their granary and root house. They spread an alarm and organized a party to pursue an Indian, supposedly a strangler of the robbing party. They brought him to the Shaffer ranch, had a trial, and hung him. Later they found that their victim had been innocent.[28]

The hanging took place near Lights Creek where North Arm joins the main part of the valley. A bridge crosses the creek and a lane provided a short cut to Taylorsville. The name Deadfall was given the bridge and lane. After the hanging, passers-by began to experience strange happenings. People said that the dead Indian was taking revenge by hanging on to carriage and wagon wheels to slow the travelers down. At other times, people claimed that they heard and even saw something behind them, only to discover that there was nothing there.[29]

The Indian Valley natives soon became well known for their peaceful nature. Old Chief Cheebeelicum and his brother Old Doc were instrumental in bringing their people back to the valley during the scare of 1858.[30]

Some areas near Indian Valley had self-appointed vigilante committees who continued to kill the Indians in their neighborhoods. In 1863, troops had been dispatched at Governor Stanford's request in response to the Hikok murders in the Mill Creek area. Should military activities bring them into the mountains, the troops were under clear order to protect the "Big Meadows" Indians, as the peaceable mountain-valley natives were called, both from hostile Indians and from unauthorized white organizations.[31]

In 1866, a small band of Mill Creeks invaded a village in Big Meadows and killed six Indians.[32] Some of the Big Meadows Indians came to Indian Valley and persuaded a few of the natives to join them in a retaliation raid. Doing so, they surprised a group of five, shot one and brought back his scalp. The evening was spent in dancing.[33]

Old Tom, one of the Indian Valley Maidu living in Honey Lake, had taken up with some Indians who looked unfamiliar to the white settlers. When asked where they came from, these natives claimed to be from Indian Valley. The settlers soon became aware of the fact that Old Tom had been going from ranch to ranch when the men were away and demanding that the women give him powder, caps, and tea lead. His so-called Indian Valley friends were "wild" Indians from northwestern Nevada and Old Tom was selling them ammunition to use in their raids against the settlers. The whites became suspicious of Old Tom when they saw skins and hides, not indigenous to this part of the country, in his possession. Five men trailed the strange Indians from Old Tom's to Papoose Valley, surprised them with an attack, and killed four bucks. Old Tom's case was discussed when they returned from the Papoose Valley raid, and several men went out to see Old Tom.

Tom escaped into the brush and the men tried to talk with him, but he refused to discuss the ammunition. He tried to call some Indians down the creek for help. John R. Perkins shot him several times when he tried to run again.. Tom ran a short distance and fell down dead.[34]

The Maidu were anxious to have peaceful relations with the white people and tried to urge their neighbors to do the same. Soldiers stationed on the eastern side of the mountains employed Maidu men to help them in their raids upon the Indians who were accused of troubling the Honey Lake settlers. Many of the Paiutes felt great bitterness toward the whites and Maidu because of these raids.[35]

The Indian Valley natives submitted passively to changes and made no attempt to resist the white settlers. None of the mountain Maidu were physically removed from their environment and taken to the reservations. Though the settlers claimed the most desirable arable land, they allowed the Indians to live near by in their campodees[36] singly and in groups. They experienced effects of constant growth of the white population and many remembered being chased off their land by the law or men with guns, as in the case of Shim Taylor. Shimm and his family lived in Genesee by Coppertown. He had spent much time as a lad with Jobe Taylor's family and liked to call himself Jobe Taylor. He planted the apple orchard near Coppertown and when the town became deserted after the Civil War, the Taylors continued to live there .. Not long afterwards, Doc Hall, the sheriff, asked the Indian Taylors to leave permanently.[37] Shimm and his family moved down Indian Creek, a mile northwest, to a little flat along the river, since known as Shimm's Flat. One day while preparing to go to an Indian "Big Time", he crawled under his wagon to fix it and someone shot him in the back.[38] With each move to less desirable land, dwellings had to be built, house-keeping set up, but somehow family units managed to hang together, desperately clinging to old customs.

Some customs, in the minds of the settlers, seemed most pagan. Old Dokesome brought this out when his brother died in 1862 leaving a young widow. Old Dokesome was about sixty years old at the time and claimed the widow for his wife, as was the Maidu custom. Dokesome had two wives, and the young widow brazenly joined herself to another Indian to which Dokesome demurred, but to no avail. A few days later in front of an audience, Dokesome met her near the Shaffer ranch and assailed her with a barrage of arrows until she was dead. With no comments from the spectators, Dokesome went his way.[39]

Many white men did find some of the marriage customs of the Maidu most convenient. It took just the consent of the woman to become married, and it was not long before some of the settlers became known as squaw men. Some actually took Indian women into their homes and raised the families as their own, while others accepted no responsibility for their actions. Many an Indian woman was left to support and feed her half-breed children, and the Indian community accepted those of mixed blood as their own.

Selling liquor to the Indians was illegal for many years, and white settlers ignored this. It was when Indians obtained liquor that their drinking caused them to become involved with assault upon each other. Indians were the subject of the news when murder was the result of a fracas. Old Doc, a brother of Chief Cheebeelicum, was killed in a drunken brawl by another Indian and some of the settlers tried to convict E. Viacava, who was accused of selling liquor to the Indians, for being indirectly responsible for the murder. Efforts to get a jury for the trial ended in failure.[40] However, because the majority of these mountain Maidu of Indian Valley went to great extremes to not become involved in any controversy, little was written after 1862 about their existence.

The white population grew and new communities sprung up around the valley as gold strikes were discovered and claimed. For the next forty-eight years, mining remained the main economy of the valley with farming and lumbering being secondary in importance.

Chapter IV
MINING SETTLEMENTS

Interests of the white population of Indian Valley centered on the potential of the mines. Influx of miners increased as the news of Indian Valley gold strikes spread to other areas. Miners were an individual breed of men possessed with perennial optimism that tomorrow's "take" will be richer than today's and would leave a paying claim on just a rumor of richer diggings. When these men looked beyond the placer diggings to the quartz claims in the mountains around Indian Valley they found ore rich in copper, gold, and silver. Camps mushroomed around richer claims and struggled to become prominent, but when production declined many became ghost towns overnight. As the mining boom gained tempo early in the '60s, the camps were dependent upon the well established settlement at Taylor's ranch for their supplies, equipment, and entertainment.

TAYLORSVILLE

In 1861 the settlement around Taylor's grist mills and ranch had no church or school, but included one livery stable, a butcher shop, a blacksmith, saloons, the E. D. Hosselkus dry goods and grocery store, another store, a fruit store, eight or ten dwellings, some Indian huts, two hotels, the Taylor House and the Vernon House.[1] Miners congregated in town at every opportunity and the proprietors of each hotel, Taylor and Springer, were known for their hospitality.

"Entertainment by Jobe T. Taylor" was the wording on the sign hung from the eaves of the Taylor House. Having visited the Taylor House at Christmas in 1865, Augustus R. Bidwell wrote the following about his experience:

> … the barroom, a room about 25 by 50 feet, had a stone fireplace that would take a backlog four and a half feet in diameter and five feet in length. The floor was of "puncheon" (logs hewed on three sides and bedded in the ground). The window casings were set deep in thick log walls and the double entrance doors likewise.

… Snow lay deep and wood was needed. Green spruce saw logs were dragged through the wide doorway in the barroom, the sweating team halting with noses almost in the fireplace. This means of getting wood in the winter was doubtless repeated in many frontier cabin, but the spectacle it created thrilled my childish imagination. The barroom crowd —- the snow on the flow —- the odor of the wood and of the spruce boughs (nailed to the wall for decoration) —- mingled with that of the team, resting by the bar while the logs were rolled aside so the team could be turned around and driven out!

The kitchen was presided over by "Aunt Abby", a negro mammy of slave days, and a notable character in early life of the community. Her cookies were famous with the children [sic]. And with red bandana on her head, she would often entertain them with songs of the south, accompanying herself on the guitar.[2]

Patriotism ran high and Taylor saw to it that the miners in and about the countryside had the opportunity to vote in local and national elections. After building the Vernon House in 1861, Springer and friends planned a Fourth of July celebration, characteristic of the times, and widely applauded as one of the best. The order of the day followed the program below:

Raising of National Flag at 10 o'clock together with a national Salute of 13 guns.
Procession to form at the VERNON HOUSE at half-past 10 marching to the TAYLOR HOUSE, thence to the grounds.

Ceremonies of the Ground,

National Song by the Choir

Reading of the Declaration

National Song

ORATION   National Song   POEM
National Salute of Thirty-four Guns
Formation of Procession and March to the Table
Regular Toasts   Volunteer Toasts and Responses

Afternoon Ceremonies

Volunteer Speeches

Evening Ceremonies

Fireworks and a GRAND BALL at the Vernon House [3]

(Upper) Close-up of Taylor's grist mill (left), and sawmill (right) taken around 1895 with Martha Gee (Barnes) in foreground.

(Lower) View of area around Taylor's grist and sawmill from the cemetery hill. Miller Blough's house is to the left and the school is to the far right background.

View of Taylorsville – About 1885

Large white building partly hid by trees, upper left, is the Taylor House. Long shed, center, is the barn for the oxen used in hauling logs. The Vernon House is the white building with many windows to the right.

The settlement had been called Indian Valley for several years and an argument developed over what the name of the town should be. Some citizens preferred the name Marion and others thought it should be Taylorville. It was put it to a vote and 128 voted for Taylorville[4] and five voted for Marion.[5]

The livelihood of the valley and mines depended on supplies and equipment which had to be shipped on pack trains into the valley. According to Fariss and Smith, the Plumas Turnpike Company was formed in 1860 to improve the road between American Valley and Indian Valley following a survey made by J. H. Whitlock. This toll road, with the gate at Toll Gate Creek on Grizzly Ridge, was eighteen miles long and was used until 1870.[6] During winter weather it took two days to travel to and from Quincy, and soon it was nicknamed the snowshoe route (see Figure on page 49). It left Indian Valley in a southeasterly direction four miles west of Taylorsville following Hough Creek, crossing Grizzly Ridge 2,400 feet above the valley floor, eventually reaching Quincy after a rough trip over rugged terrain.[7]

Snowshoes on Horses

Wooden snowshoes were introduced in 1865. When damp snow clung to them, iron was substituted, but later thin plates of steel with rubber linings proved most satisfactory. They were nine inches square and were fastened with screws and straps. Each shoe was fitted separately, as the feet varied in size. It took two hours to put shoes on a four horse team.

Jobe Taylor surveyed a new trail in 1861 which cut six miles off the turnpike The Taylor trail left his ranch in a southerly direction intersection the Hough Creek road two and a half miles away. Taylor let the contract to the Chinese for $1000 and they failed to complete the road so Taylor and J.W. Thompson did the work themselves.[8]

With a string of horses and some cash, John Hartgrave purchased the Vernon House from E.D Springer in 1864. The Hartgraves ran the hotel, engaged in the freighting business and promoted the Red Clover Road from Taylorsville, Genesee, east along Red Clover Creek, through Beckwourth Pass to Reno. This road materialized in 1870 and eventually became the main Indian Valley – Reno road. As mining activity increased, new roads were periodically proposed, but because of lack of funds few became realities.

Vernon House and Hartgrave Red Clover – Reno Stage – 1900

COPPERTOWN

The Reward Mine on the mountain west of the Fred Borden place provided enough copper ore to cause John Chapman to build a smelter in the early 1860's near the confluence of Grizzly and Indian Creeks in Genesee. Ore was hauled by ox team to the smelter which was operated by charcoal made in the valley. The smelter blower was driven by a water wheel, thirty feet in diameter. A community, sometimes called Chapmanville, grew around the smelter. The Reward Mine ran out of rich ore, the price of copper went down, and when the mine closed down after 1865, the smelter was abandoned. A man named Wheaton homesteaded the Coppertown field and later sold it to E.D. Hosselkus.[9]

ROUND VALLEY

One of the earliest pack trails, possibly an Indian trail, came from Big Meadows to Indian Valley, up to Round Valley, thence to Long Valley and down Rush Creek to Rich Bar. This was the route Lassen and Bruff followed when they launched their Gold Lake search. Gold-bearing ledges had been discovered as early as 1851 in the mountains along the northwestern end of Indian Valley. In 1856, J. W. Ellis relocated the Bullion Ledge found by Cornelison in 1851, and the Ellis mine at Round Valley. Placer gold was discovered by Palmer and Newlands on the west slope of North Canyon in 1860. In 1861 the successes of these ledges attracted many people to Round Valley and it soon became one of the liveliest camps in the state.

In 1862, E.W. Judkins was averaging $175 a day from the sixteen-stamp Golden Gate Mill. The valley began to echo constant rumbling of arastras and poundings of stamp mills, the old and new way of crushing the ore-bearing rock.

A constant supply of water was a necessity for the stamp mills, mines, and sawmills. Round Valley basin appeared to be a natural setting for a reservoir and the narrow outlet at the head of north Canyon seemed ideal for a dam. C.E. Lawrence let a contract to John W. Ellis to build the first Round Valley dam in 1862.[10] It was completed and in the following spring, a fourteen foot dam of rough two-by-four and double one-by-twelve boards broke when the water rose beyond seven feet. The flood revealed pay gravel in the canyon and claims were immediately staked.[11] Work in rebuilding the dam was started so that the '63 spring run-off could be stored. The new dam was a rock and dirt filled log crib dam intended to store about twenty feet of water. It turned out that the spillway was too narrow and shallow, and this dam broke causing a flood of such great proportions that huge scars from it remained for several decades. The bridges were washed out in Greenville at Chinatown and Crescent Streets, and further down the valley at Arlington beyond Crescent Mills.[12]

By the end of 1863, the town boasted a steam saw mill turning out 8,000 feet of lumber per day, three large stores, a Wells Fargo Office, and a hotel called Silica House. The population was 300 men, 28 women, and 50 children. With the settlement growing so fast, the following advertisement was placed in the Plumas Standard:[13]

WANTED

To grace our city

A good physician. A good barber. A good cobbler. Any good thing.

Freight was shipped to Round Valley from the settlements in the Sacramento Valley from Marysville through Buck's Ranch, Meadow Valley, Quincy, then over the road maintained by the Plumas Turnpike Company to Indian Valley and on up Dixie Canyon to Round Valley. This route from Quincy seemed most circuitous, so in the spring of 1863, the more direct Shaffer trail was repaired for $1000, and O.D. Peck was appointed road overseer for the valley. The trail came down Dixie Canyon from Round Valley and followed Indian Creek thence over the mountains at Shoo Fly to Black Hawk near Quincy.[14] Though this trail appeared to have a gentler grade than the one over Grizzly, it was not until 1866 that road builders asked for county support. The construction commenced but the voters failed to support the measure, and contractor William H. Blood died after finishing but a few miles. In 1870, the State legislature authorized the county to issue bonds in the amount of $20,000 for the completion of the road. A.W. Keddie surveyed the route and W.G. Young and M.S. Bransford did the construction work which included building the Shoo Fly Bridge below Indian Falls.[15]

Before the ledges played out at Round Valley, the name Silica was adopted for the town.[16] By 1870 most of the businesses had moved to Greenville, which was quickly becoming an important settlement in the valley.

Remembering the years just before Round Valley was abandoned, J.J.L. Peel wrote about his experience as part-owner of the Ellis placer and quartz mines. Frank Mahan and Peel were partners, each cleaning up about $20 to $50 each day. E.W. Judkins brought some investors from San Francisco who offered Peel and Mahan $100,000 for the property. They accepted the offer, but before the agreement was signed, saloon keeper Nick Trucks advised Mahan to hold out for a higher price. Failure to sell culminated in leasing the property to Judkins who succeeded in forming the Round Valley Mining Company with Mahan, Peel, Alex Tate, Alex Knisely, L.G. Traugh, Benjamin Harvey, and E.D. Hosselkus as stockholders. There were two quartz mills, sixteen stamps at Round Valley and twelve stamps in North Canyon. All went well at first, but soon got off the pay streak, ran out of money, and owed much in the valley for castings and machinery. The creditors leveled an attachment and closed the entire plant with wages due all of the men. Twelve hundred dollars were owed to the chief engineer, Matt Johnson. The men were furious and threatened violence when Traugh, the president, arrived astride a scrawny pony. Everyone was surprised to see him on such a bag of bones, as he had owned a fine riding horse. He said that he had sold it for a fine wad of gold which he had in his pocket and there it would stay. Johnson's furor rose beyond control and soon the camp was startled by the sound of blows on the machinery made with a heavy sledge. Johnson damaged the machinery at both mills beyond repair before anyone could stop him. He managed to escape ahead of the posse to Montana where it was reported that he made a fortune.[17]

GREENVILLE

Fariss and Smith state that the first house in Greenville, at the foot of North Canyon, was built in 1862 by Alfred McCargar. However, the town was named after John Winthrop Green[18], whose wife served meals to the miners, and their log cabin was known as Green's Hotel. The family lived there for a year or two and moved to Marysville.[19] By the summer of 1863, the town was growing rapidly and there were quite a number of residences built, including that of Henry C. Bidwell, who became known as the father of Greenville because of his many interests and investments in the community. The town soon supported Mr. Lynn's hotel, Bidwell's boarding house, a blacksmith, a brewery, Bidwell's general merchandise store, McBeth and Compton's store, Wells Fargo & Co., a foundry, Lawrence's sawmill, a livery stable, and I. C. Patch's flour mill (see Figures on page 53). By 1867, two hundred miners were guaranteed employment in the Greenville area.[20]

The McBeth & Compton building is the present site of F. L. Miller & Company. The brick bank building has housed a butcher shop and with a stucco covering is the present location of Vern Weinrich's barber shop.

Main Street of Greenville – Around 1885

Near Greenville in North Canyon was a quartz mill at the Westcott Mine, later known as the New York, which was operated by the first pressure type Pelton wheel in the region. It was a crude affair run by water shot through a canvas hose. The wheel soon became known as a "hurdy gurdy" throughout the region.

Touring "ladies" provided entertainment for the men in the camps. There were usually four in a group attended by a male escort, the "master of ceremonies". They would spend a week in each camp and local fiddlers provided the music for the dancing parties. If fiddlers were not available the escort would play a small hand organ known as a hurdy-gurdy and the dancers were known as "hurdy-gurdies". Greenville's social standards were not very high in those days, but when the girls were given accommodations at the Greenville hotel, it was enough to stir up the few women in the town. Once they held an indignation meeting and decided positively that the "hurdy-gurdies" were NOT to "run the hotel".[21]

Greenville had its Chinatown and the Chinese provided most of the help in the boarding houses around the mining camps. They were excellent cooks and many remained as permanent help with some of the families, the Firmstones, the Bidwells, and the Hoselkuses, for many years. The people of Greenville did not like the name of Chinatown, so they renamed it Bradford Addition.[22] Since the Chinese were prohibited from working the better claims, they would quietly work an abandoned placer claim and often do quite well.

In 1863 the Chico Humboldt Wagon Road had been completed as far as Big Meadows. For $5,000 a Mr. Ellis promoted a road north from Greenville following Wolf Creek and eventually connecting with the Chico road near Prattville at Big Meadows.[23] The road was eventually completed with a toll bridge, owned by H. C. Bidwell, on the North Fork of the Feather River at Nevis Island. In 1866, H. C. Bidwell sold his interest in this new toll road to General Bidwell of Chico.[24] The route became the preferred for express and freight, as it was only seventy miles to Bidwell's Landing, on the Sacramento river, from Greenville. Late spring snows did not discourage the freight companies in 1867 as goods for Taylorsville were shipped from Sacramento Valley by wagons to the snow, over the snow to Humbug on sleighs, from Humbug to within a half a mile of Taylorsville on mules, crossed the river on boats, and thence by wagons to Taylorsville.[25]

CHEROKEE

The Kittle ledge discovered in Cherokee Ravine in 1865 was one of the richest strikes during the Indian Valley mining boom of the 60's. Glazier & Company built the largest quartz mill in the county, at that time, near the claim.[26] The Kittle Mining Company was formed with foreign interests from London and proposed to build a steam hoist and pumping plant as further development of the claim. In 1864 the Caledonia was discovered next to the Kittle and water pumped from the shafts of these two mines was used in the mill.

The Kittle Mining Company also acquired the rights to the Round Valley Basin and made plans to build a new dam in 1864 in time for water storage in 1865. This third dam was constructed with considerable planning and expense. A rock wall twenty feet at the base was laid between bedrock abutments and was twenty-five feet high. An immense dirt fill was placed in front of the wall and an outlet pipe was laid through the center. This dam proved trustworthy for many years to come. Because none of the trees had been removed from the basin, the reservoir was full of floating debris and foul water for years.

The Cherokee camp, a saloon, a Compton store, and the Welfare Hotel developed around the mills of these two rich mines to meet the needs of the miners. George and Mary Ann Bellas ran the hotel, and "Mother" Bellas gave many a hard luck miner charitable sympathy well spiced with sound Irish advice. Along with its neighbor, Round Valley, Cherokee became a ghost town in 1870. Most of the equipment from the mills was moved to other claims, and the buildings were removed to Greenville.[27]

WOLF CREEK

Gold was discovered on a tributary of Wolf Creek about four miles west of Greenville, and in 1865 Wagonner and Vanscile reported that they were getting $20 to $50 per ton from their quartz mill.[28] The mine produced steadily, and a small settlement remained there for many years. The main mine, The Gold Stripe, had thirty-nine stamps going in 1880.

ARLINGTON

In the southwestern corner of Indian Valley the main wagon toad crossed Indian Creek, and it was here that the Arlington settlement grew. Bridges were built only to be washed out during years when the spring run-off was excessive. In the spring of 1862, John Pattinger built a toll bridge across the creek and with the permission of the county supervisors was permitted to operate a ferry until the bridge was completed.[29] Unfortunately, with the breaking of the Round Valley dam the following spring, the bridge was washed away again. Since the bridge was on the main wagon road to Round Valley, Greenville, and Big Meadows, it was rebuilt.

Logging in Taylorsville – 1872

The settlement was small at Arlington, and before Crescent Mills became established as a town, it had the county hospital, a zinc mine, and Matt Knoll's brewery. The saw mill and quartz mill at Dixie Canyon were but a short distance away (see Map on page 59).

CRESCENT MILLS

The richest claim around Indian Valley and one to remain productive for many years was the Green Mountain Mine discovery on the ridge above Cherokee (see Map on page 59). The Crescent and Monitor claims were located in the same vicinity. In 1866, the town of Crescent Mills was a thriving camp rivaling Greenville in size.

Additional water was needed for milling and steam power, and in 1867 the eight-mile water ditch was built from the Kittle at Round Valley to Crescent Mills. A spur, less than two miles in length, was built to the Indian Valley mine between Crescent Mills and Greenville.[30]

Crescent Mills, in 1880, had the largest quartz mills in the valley. The Green Mountain mills had ninety-one stamps which often operated day and night. The other mills in the valley were smaller with the following number of stamps: Indian Valley, fifty-six; Gold Stripe, thirty-nine; Plumas National, thirty; Kittle, twenty; New York, ten; Crescent, thirty-two; and the Monitor, ten.[31]

Mining was at a peak; however, veins began to play out and activity gradually slowed down. The bank in Greenville failed in December of 1882 and the manager, E. Prowattain, was thought to have embezzled the funds, but a lack of evidence caused the judge to find him not guilty.[32]

The next year, the Plumas National, reported signs of a depression and many of the mines continued to produce, but were constantly changing owners. In November, 1885, the Cherokee Gold Mining Company, including the Kittle, Caledonia, and Summit quartz mines were up for sale and in 1887 the Ellis quartz claim and the Green Mountain appeared in the same section of advertisements. The year before, 1886, the effects of hydraulic mining had caused citizens of Sutter County to instigate suits against one hundred and twenty mining companies of Plumas County.[33]

For the next few years' activity increased and Greenville became the largest community in the valley with a population of six hundred people. Crescent Mills was the next in size with four hundred. There was talk of a Big Meadows dam and, with a railroad and timber interests growing, a prosperous future was expected. It was predicted that when the railroad came through the mountains and speculation ran high as to where, that John H. Smith would make a fortune on his ten acre ice pond.[34]

Portion of 1866 Plumas County Map, V. Wackenrender,
surveyor under State Geologist, J. D. Whitney.

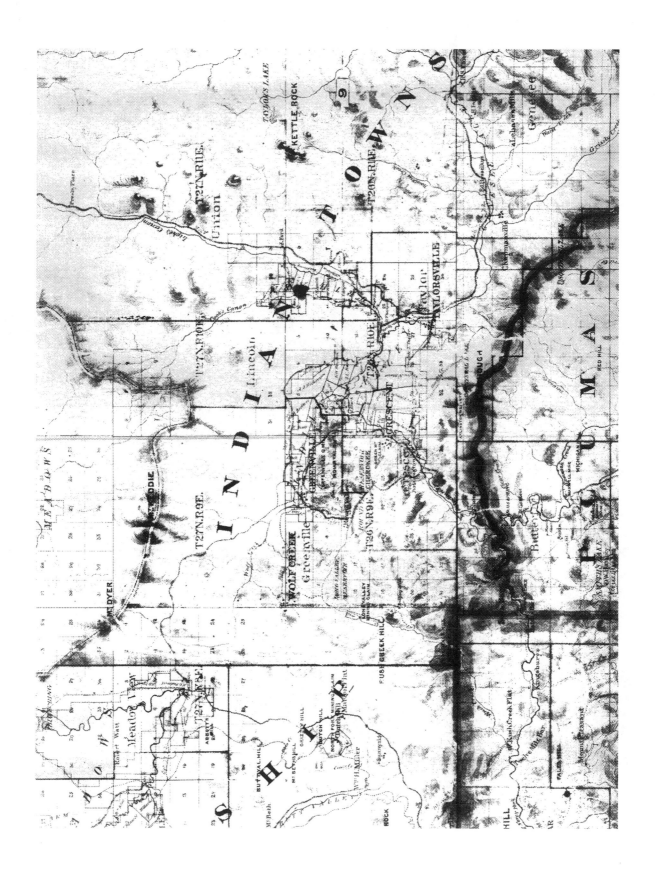

59

Portion of Keddie's Map of Plumas County, California. Compiled and Published by Arthur W. Keddie, C. E., U. S. Deputy & Licensed Land Surveyor for California, Quincy, California.

Adopted and Declared the Official Map of Plumas County by
Resolution of the Board of Supervisors, March 8, 1892.

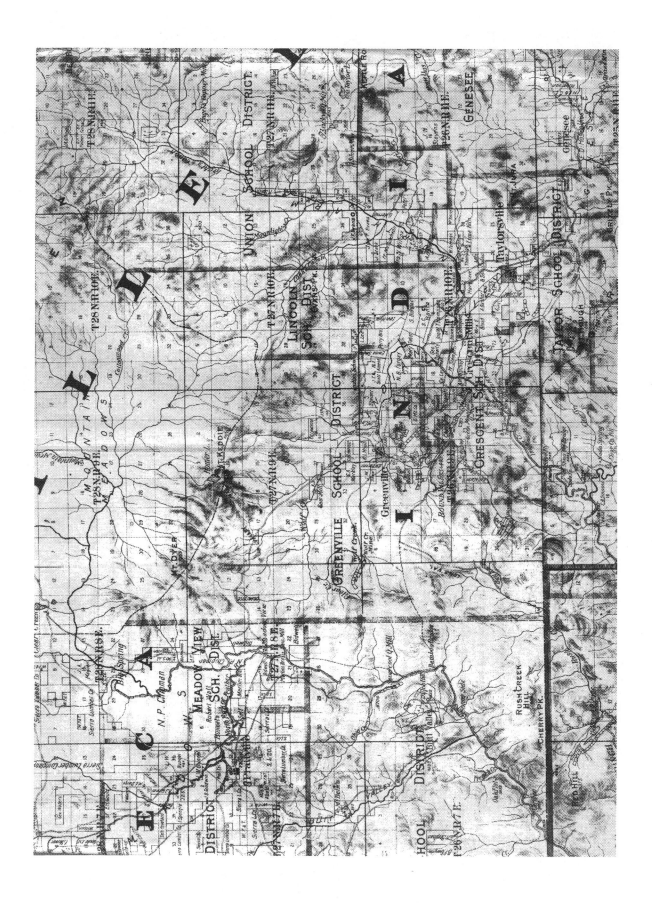

Chapter V
ACCULTURATION OF THE INDIANS

Prior to the middle eighties the Maidu of Indian Valley had done little to assimilate themselves into the white way of life. True, they provided much of the manual labor on the ranches and were considered most dependable. They wore the white man's clothes and learned to speak English. But many a settler thought the Indians to be dirty, beggarly, ignorant and unfit to be his equal. Nothing was provided to help the Indian to better himself and in 1884 only three Indians were attending school in Plumas County.[1] In all, they were tolerated as long as they performed a service in the white economy. On the other hand, some curious settlers provided themselves with entertainment by visiting and eating with the Indian in his campodee, observing the "Big Times" or "Indian Sunday" from a distance, or actually taking part in sweating ceremonies.[2]

The federal government expressed concern on the status of the American Indian on reservations as it was discovered that reservation life fostered indolence and perpetuated Indian customs which held Indians back from assimilation. Therefore, on February 8, 1887, Congress passed the Dawes Act, known as the Allotment Act, which authorized the president to divide the reservations into individual parcels and to give every Indian a piece of tribally-owned land.[3] The land was to be held in trust for 25 years, after which a patent in fee simple would devolve upon the individual. With it would go all the rights and duties of citizenship. Tribal land remaining after the allotments was declared surplus, and the president was authorized to open it to non-Indian homesteaders, the Indians being paid the homestead price. Upon passage of this Act, about two-thirds of the Indian lands in the United States left Indian ownership.

Even though the northern Maidu of Indian Valley lacked a tight tribal organization and did not live on a reservation, some of the Indians received allotments in the acreage according to law.[4] The agent handling the allotments interpreted the act to mean each full-blooded Indian and those with white blood were denied the allotment privilege, as in the case of Daisy Meadows Baker, Rosie Meadows Salem, and their brother Joaquin

Meadows. All had been born before the Dawes Act, but it was claimed that their father had been a white man, and the agent called them white, not Indian. The girls had been raised by their pure-blooded Indian grandmother and grandfather and were raised in the Maidu custom and tradition. These and others constituted the large group of landless Indians in California.

Chico Jim was ready to make his claim to an allotment, as he was one Indian who had trained himself to become a farmer and had put his land under cultivation before the act. When the act became law, he had "Final Proof of continuous residence and cultivation of land" published in the Greenville Bulletin with prominent settlers, J.S. Peck, C.H. Martin, David Thompson, and Isaac Hall as witnesses.[5] The Chico Jim cemetery on the eastern side of the valley originated on this land.

Most of the Indians who received parcels of land had no conception of what should be done with the land. Some of the Indian Valley natives moved about following the haying season, clearing land, and building fences. These Indians were seasonal crews and would set up temporary structures for living quarters.

Daisy Baker remembers that her husband worked at many ranches in Indian Valley and also at the Hosselkus ranch in Genesee. Sometime around 1900, the Bakers went to live along the northern edge of Genesee on the parcel received by Mr. Baker as his allotment. He built a fine log cabin for his wife and three children. Soon afterwards there was a small-pox epidemic and Mr. Baker and two of the children contracted the disease. Two people on the south side of the valley died from the disease, and the Baker family was able to pull through the sickness. Before their complete recovery, though, white men came along and burned their cabin, leaving them with nothing, not even an explanation for their actions. Daisy said that no other cabin or house was burned, though many people were sick with the disease. Bill, her husband, soon built them a smaller cabin near the site of the first one, but they did not stay there long. They went back to Indian Valley and Lilly was born near *ko-sim* at a place called *pa-toot*. A few years later they moved to Honey Lake Valley where Mr. Baker was murdered.[6]

In 1926 Rollin Baker, one of the sons, wrote the Indian Agency questioning them about his father's allotment. The following letter was the reply from the Agency (see Figure on page 62):

My dear friend:-

This will acknowledge receipt of your letter of Jan. 13th requesting information concerning the allotment of your father, Billy Baker, deceased , Susanville Allottee 418.

Kindly be advised that your father filed application for allotment in Genesee Valley, described as SE/4 of NW/4, S/2 of NE/4. Sec. 11, and SW/4 of NW/4, Sec. 12 Twp. 25 N., R 11E., containing 160 acres. However, it appears that same was cancelled on

Dec. 17, 1901, on relinquishment presumably signed by Billy Baker. Your father always denied that he signed the relinquishment and before his death steps were being taken to secure affidavits that would prove he made certain improvements on the land. It seems that James T Taylor and George E. Boyden have knowledge of the facts in this case. However, we have not been able to secure affidavits from them and until such affidavits are secured from either them or other parties who know the facts in the case it will be impossible to re-establish any claim that your father may have to the land.

Your friend,

(signed) L. A. Dorrington, Supt.

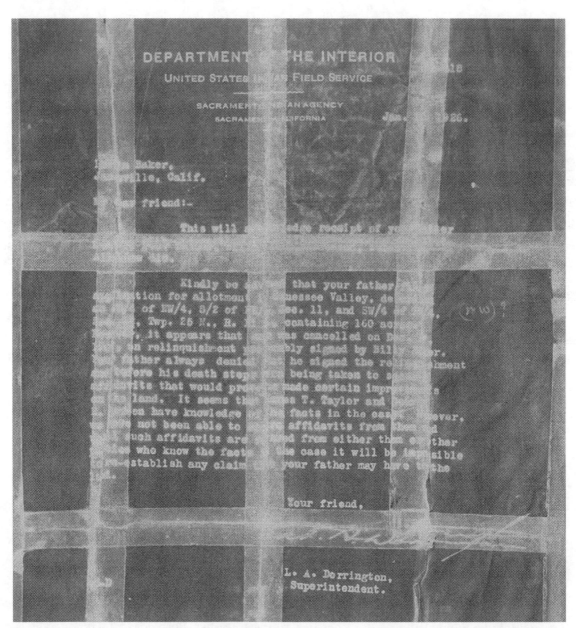

Copy of January 21, 1925 letter to Rollin Baker from the Department of the Interior, United States Indian Field Service, Sacramento Indian Agency, Sacramento, California

According to the law, once an Indian received his allotment, it was his for 25 years and during that time he had no right as a citizen to sell it or even give it away. Rollin did not pursue the matter any further, as most Indians lacked understanding of their own rights as citizens and were unable to protect themselves against violations by federal, state and county governments and individuals.

The surplus land was sold to homesteaders and a few local settlers took advantage of this opportunity to get land.

It was hoped that the Allotment Act would give the Indian automatic acculturation. The result was a weakening of native institutions and cultural practices with nothing offered in its place. Those who supported the act felt that the Indians would gradually die out, thereby dissolving the problem, but the reverse was true. Help began in the 90's when some of the local citizens began to do something about assimilation, by helping Indians learn non-Indian ways.

INDIAN MISSION

Two stories, which probably are the same without proper sequence of events, exist as to the first school for Indian children in Indian Valley. A.R. Bidwell wrote[7] that Charley Hall, related to the Isaac Hall family, was working on the Hall ranch and gathered some Indians together to start a Sunday School. With the help of the Indians he built a log cabin and was determined he would teach them to read and sing. He set a date, and invited the local ranchers to visit his school. When they arrived, Hall went out to greet his guests only to return to an empty building. His pupils had fled during his brief absence, and Hall became the victim of many jokes. He was not discouraged, and soon the Methodist Board of Missions lent its assistance. A site was secured, and temporary buildings were built with Edgar N. Ament and his wife in charge.[8] The government later took it over as a unit of the Indian School System.

According to a clipping of an unidentified paper, 1897, a school for Indian children was started by Mrs. Amelia Martin in her home. Edgar Ament took it over, enlarged it, and through him the Indian School was established under the auspices of the federal government and Women's National Indian Association. In 1897, it was known as the Greenville Indian Industrial Boarding School, and Ament was the officer in charge. The school consisted of a water supply, a dormitory, store house, school house, and chapel. There were sixty pupils at the school, and they represented several California tribes.

Church groups maintained missions for the Indians in California and someone finally called upon the federal government for help. Their answer was the purchase of Rancherias or home sites for California landless Indians. The Rancherias were small and on poor land, but still owned by the government.[9] It was then that the federal government acquired forty acres of the School from the Women's National Indian Association and later the government added one hundred and sixty acres in 1902, and seventy-five acres in 1916.[10] The purpose of the school was part of the federal plan of Indian education to prepare Indian youth for duties, privileges, and responsibilities of American citizenship. The students had to be at least one-fourth Indian, and no parent able to pay for their education could send their children to the school.

The two-story dormitory burned in 1897, and the students were able to lodge in the schoolhouse while new accommodations were built. The home was owned by the National Indian Association and used by the federal government's Indian Training School.

The school continued to enlarge and improvements were periodically made by local contractors with crews of Indian workmen. In 1906 contractor W.W. Blood employed Indians to build new buildings and enlarge the reservoirs.[11] John Hardgrave and his father held the government contract for many years to provide the school with produce from their vegetable garden.[12]

The Rev. J.M. Johnson was pastor of the school in 1907. There were eighty pupils at the school, and he made a trip to the Sacramento Valley to secure more in the hope of increasing the enrollment to one hundred.[13] He soon preached his last sermon to the largest congregation ever to get together at the school, and the subject was on legal marriage. The success of the sermon culminated in the marriage of Abro Johnson and Mary Washoe, who had lived together for four years.[14] The Indians had a grand time during the occasion and it was said that Abro was willing to go through with the ceremony, but Mary needed much persuasion.[15]

C.T. Coggeshall, from the general office of the U.S. Indian Service, Washington, D.C., succeeded Dr. W.Q. Tucker as superintendent in 1909. Upon his arrival all of the Indians in the valley were invited for a powwow to discover what the government had in store for them. The attendance was large and Coggeshall explained to them that the buildings were run down and that there was some talk of the government giving up the school because the Indians lacked interest in it. He told them that the government wanted help and wanted the Indians to send their children to the school. They had planned baseball for the boys, basketball for the girls, and a brass band. He asked them to be proud of their race. Soon thereafter they had a farm school, and the girls learned to do lovely beadwork. The baseball team from the Indian School was the arch rival of the Greenville team.[16]

During that year, Greenville was the first community in the valley to get electricity through the efforts of the Indian Valley Light and Power Company, and in July, 1910, the Indian School was wired and received power. Another fire destroyed the barn and several small buildings at a loss of $2,000.

In 1911, Congress, through efforts of Representative E. Baker of Susanville, appropriated $30,000 to the Mission School which was proportioned in the following manner: $4,000 for the Superintendent's residence; $1,200 for the shop building for instruction of blacksmith work; $7,000 for the school farm; $6,000 for the school and assembly buildings; and $5,000 for heating equipment for all the buildings.[17]

There were one hundred and forty-eight pupils in 1918, but only ten graduates, according to the school's annual calendar. Shortly thereafter, in 1922, the school burned again, never to be rebuilt because the government was becoming interested in fewer schools. The children from the Rancheria began to attend the nearby Lincoln School with the white children.

END OF SOME SOCIAL PRACTICES

The first decade of the century saw an end to many of the customs and practices of these northeastern Maidu. It was fortunate for posterity that from 1899 to 1903, a small group of anthropologists under the auspices of the Huntington California expedition spent part of each year in Indian and Genesee Valleys to record as much as they could of the language, habits, and customs of these people.[18] The men boarded with the Hosselkus family on their ranch in Genesee and spent much of their time with the head men of the tribe. Herbert Young remembers that when men were getting $1.00 a day for haying and working on clearing land, his father, Tom Young, received $2.00 from Dixon. Young supplied nineteen of the twenty-one myths from Genesee in Dixon's collection of "Maidu Myths".[19]

The last sweat houses disappeared, but the practice of sweating went on makeshift brush huts. The Indians never completely accepted the marriage customs of the white man, and it caused many problems among their own people when inheritance was a factor. Burials were always carried off in Indian fashion in terms of position of the body and the water was put in a beaded bottle instead of a basket. Burning of the deceased's possessions degenerated to the burning of only those articles which were highly favored by the deceased. Wailing at funerals eventually ceased for the younger generation, but the older people found it a necessary release of the emotions. Gambling continued in milder forms as possessions were few.

"Burnings" held usually in October to honor the dead of the past two or three years eventually stopped. It was rare when mourning was carried on more than ten or fifteen years, so when the last "burning" was held in Genesee around 1910, the circumstances were most unusual. Comencie, or Mrs. Shim Taylor, then close to ninety years old, brought her son's body from Oroville to bury him where he was born. The son had died thirty years before, but Comencie grieved as though it were yesterday.[20] Comencie had a lovely big basket whose design depicted the rays of the rising sun. It was made for the burning, but Mr. Rosebury of Susanville was able to bribe her husband, and he sold the basket to Roseberry. It was thought that Comencie never realized that the basket was not burned during that last ceremony.

Few Maidu maintained the custom, but attempts have been made to perpetuate some of the lore, games, big times, and basket making. Daisy Baker continues to make baskets, but the younger generation show little desire to learn the craft. However, as babies arrive Daisy receives requests to provide them with traditional baby baskets. A spring bear dance was held in Honey Lake Valley in 1962 and was attended by Maidu and Paiutes of the area. Herbert Young performed the singing as the shaman. But the oldsters refused to dance and complained that those who danced were not doing it properly. Recordings were made of songs and games so the younger generation may have them.

Thus we find the Maidu of today caught between the culture of the dying generation and that of the white man today. He recognizes that he has come from a populous people who have aided materially to the progress and wealth of Indian Valley. He has lifted himself above his primitive ancestors by his own efforts, seldom aided, often hindered by the white man. He sees around him a white man's culture; he wants to, and he knows he must enter it.

No doubt further research with those Indians maintaining their customs and careful scientific investigation of the archaeological sites may enhance our knowledge of not only the Indian Valley Indians, but those of California and the Great Basin area. The Indians' present status in the local communities might be better understood and improved as the result of further studies.

Notes

Chapter I

1. (9), p. 717.
2. (33), p. 11.
3. United States Forest Service, Rainfall Record, Greenville District, California.

Chapter II

1. (9), pp. 366, 435, and 443.
2. (39).
3. (15), p. 282.
4. (7), p. 392.
5. (7), linguistic map.
6. (10), p.19.
7. (22), p. 35.
8. (7), p. 399.
9. (22), p. 35.
10. (23), p. 131.
11. Roland B. Dixon spent much time in 1899 with the northeastern Maidu and gathered much of the information from Herbert Young's father in Genesee Valley.
12. (7), p. 393.
13. (7), p. 398.
14. (22), p. 35.
15. (9), p. 549.
16. (10), pp. 60 – 61.
17. (7), pp. 408 – 409.
18. (40).
19. (7), p. 405.
20. (23), p. 187.
21. (36) and (37).
22. (23), p. 189..

23. (23), p. 189.
24. (36) and (37).
25. (10), pp. 50–51.
26. (9), p. 370
27. (9), pp. 197–199.
28. (23), pp. 181–184.
29. (10), pp. 48–49.
30. (10), p. 68.
31. (10), p. 38.
32. (23), p. 192.
33. (10), p. 39.
34. (25), p. 191.
35. (10), p. 49.
36. (7), p. 410.
37. (10), pp. 43–46.
38. (38), April 1, 1963.
39. (10), p. 46.
40. (10), p. 66.
41. (7), p. 414.
42. (7), p. 418.
43. (10), pp. 70–73.
44. (5), p. 269.
45. (18), p. 67.
46. (18), p. 72.
47. (37).
48. (18), p. 73.
49. (10), p. 89.
50. (10), p. 89.
51. (36) and (37).
52. (10), p. 96.
53. (7), p. 416.
54. (16), pp. 75–76.
55. (11), pp. 15, 31.
56. (36) and (37).
57. (5), p. 399.
58. (10), p. 143.
59. (23), p. 229.
60. (23), p. 230.

61. (7), p. 428.
62. (36) and (37).
63. (10), p. 119.
64. (22), pp. 32–6
65. (20), pp. 268–9.
66. (35).
67. (39), April 1, 1963.
68. (23), pp. 264–6.

Chapter III

1. (3), p. 145.
2. (9), p. 367.
3. (9), p. 444.
4. (9), p. 446.
5. (9), p. 455.
6. Later called the Isadore; owners thereafter were W.T. Ward, A.J. Hickerson, and the Hannon brothers, present owners.
7. (3), p. 295.
8. (28), October 8, 1936, p. 1.
9. (3), p. 299.
10. (3), pp. 295 – 6.
11. (28), October 13, 1936, p. 1.
12. Charlie Shunam's wife was Lucy Baker, sister to Lilly Baker's grandfather, Baker Bill.
13. (26), pp. 30–1.
14. (1), PP. 489–90.
15. (1), pp. 477–8.
16. (3), pp. 213–4.
17. (6), pp. 58–9.
18. (3), pp. 213–4.
19. (3), p. 296.
20. (3), pp. 156–60.
21. (4), p. 18.
22. (4), pp. 25–26.
23. (29), November 25, 1858, pp. 3–4.
24. (4), p. 13.
25. (4), pp. 83–88.
26. (28), October 8, 1936, p. 1.

27.   (29), April 29, 1858, p. 2.

28.   (28), October 8, 1936, p. 1.

29.   (38), April 1, 1936.

30.   (27), February 9, 1887, p. 2.

31.   (8), pp. 68–9.

32.   (31), August 18, 1866, p. 2.

33.   (31), November 19, 1866, p. 2.

34.   (4), pp. 397–9.

35.   (16), pp. 9–10.

36.   Paiute name for an Indian camp, commonly used by the white settlers when speaking of any Indian dwelling or camp.

37.   (37), Selina Jackson, who still lives in Oroville, remembers being run off the Coppertown field when a young child.

38.   (38), April 1, 1963.

39.   (32), July 30, 1862, p. 3.

40.   (27), February 9, 1887, p. 2.

Chapter IV

1.   (41), Ruth Taylor's diary of 1861.

2.   (28), 1936–37.

3.   (32), June 29, 1861, p. 5.

4.   An s has been added since, and the town is called Taylorsville.

5.   (32), January 3, 1863, p. 3

6.   (3), p. 234.

7.   (31), May 18, 1867, p. 3.

8.   (32), January 3, 1863, p. 3.

9.   (24), p. 8.

10.   (32), February 28, 1862.

11.   (29), January 10, 1936, p. 1.

12.   (32). February 7, 1863, p. 2.

13.   (32), February 7, 1863, p. 2.

14.   (32), May 9, June 20, 1863, p. 3.

15.   (3), p. 235.

16.   (32), February 7, 1863, p.2.

17.   Written by J.J.L Peel in 1917.

18.   Green's first name was provided in a letter by Green's granddaughter, August, 1962, to Barbara Standard who sent it to Mrs. Bruce Bidwell.

19.   Notes written by A.R. Bidwell.

20.   (31), April 27, 1867, p. 3.
21.   (280), February 13, 1936, p. 1.
22.   Notes written by A.R. Bidwell.
23.   (32), October 4, 1862, p. 3.
24.   (31), November 24, 1866, p. 3.
25.   (31), May 18, 1867, p. 3.
26.   (32), November 29, 1863, p. 2.
27.   (28), February 20, 1936, p. 1.
28.   (32), November 29, 1863, p. 3.
29.   (32), March 29, 1863, p. 3.
30.   (31), April 27, 1867, p. 3.
31.   (27), October 6, 1880, p. 3.
32.   (31), December 9, 1882, p. 3.
33.   (31), April 30, 1887, p. 3.
34.   (27), December 26, 1888, p. 2.

Chapter V

1.   (31), December 13, 1884, p. 3.
2.   Harley Flourney and J.J.L. Peel both write of these experiences.
3.   See Appendix for the basic elements of the Act.
4.   Many present-day Indians feel that the Act stated that each Indian was to get 160 acres.
5.   (31) May 4, 1887, p. 2..
6.   (36) and (37).
7.   Letter written to his daughter, Elsie Bumgardner of Oroville.
8.   Edgar N. Ament lived on the Ament ranch, formerly the Hall ranch, and later became the mayor of Berkeley, California.
9.   (14), p. 10.
10.   Letter from the Bureau of Indian Affairs, May 10, 1963, (See Appendix).
11.   (30), November 30, 1906, p. 5.
12.   John Hardgrave.
13.   (30), October 18, 1907, p. 8.
14.   (30), October 18, 1907, p. 8.
15.   (36) and (37).
16.   (30), September 24, 1909, p. 1.
17.   Correspondence from Mrs. Mary Dunn, Quincy, California, April 5, 1963.
18.   (23), p. 121.
19.   (40).
20.   (17), Plate 4

BIBLIOGRAPHY

BOOKS

(1)   Brancroft, H. H. <u>History of California, VII 1860-1890.</u> San Francisco: The History Company, 1890. 826 pp.

(2)   Brewer, William H. <u>Up and Down California in 1860-1864.</u> New Haven: Yale University Press, 1930. 601 pp.

(3)   Fariss and Smith (publishers). <u>Illustrated History of Lassen, Sierra, and Plumas Counties from 1530 to 1850.</u> San Francisco: Fariss and Smith, 1882. 507 pp.

(4)   Fairfield, Asa Merrill. <u>Pioneer History of Lassen County.</u> San Francisco: H.S. Crocker Company, 1916. 506 pp.

(5)   Heizer, R.F. and M.A, Whipple (eds.). <u>The California Indians:</u> A Source Book. Berkeley: University of California Press, 1960. 492 pp.

(6)   Hittell, T.H. <u>History of California, IV.</u> San Francisco: N.J. Stone & Co., 1897.

(7)   Kroeber, A.L. <u>Handbook of the Indians of California.</u> Berkeley: California Book Co., Ltd. 1935. 995 pp.

(8)   Kroeber, Theodora. <u>Ishi in Two Worlds.</u> Berkeley: University of California Press, 1961.

(9)   Read, Georgia W. and Ruth Gaines (eds.). <u>Gold Rush: The Journals, Drawings, and Other Papers of J. Goldsborough Bruff, April 2, 1849 – July 20, 1851.</u> New York: Columbia University Press.

(10)   Schultz, Paul E. <u>Indians of Lassen Volcanic National Park and Vicinity.</u> Mineral, California: Loomis Museum Association, Lassen Volcanic National Park, 1954. 176 pp.

PUBLICATIONS OF THE GOVERNMENT, LEARNED SOCIETIES, AND OTHER ORGANIZATIONS

(11)   Davis, James T. "Trade Routes and Economic Exchange Among the Indians of California," <u>Reports of the University of California Archaeological Survey,</u>" No. 54. Berkeley: Department of Anthropology, University of California, 1961.

(12)   Elsasser, Albert B. "Aboriginal Use of Restrictive Sierran Environments," <u>Reports of the University of California Archaeological Survey</u>, No. 41 Berkeley: Department of Anthropology, University of California, n.d.

(13)   Elsasser, Albert B. "The Archaeology of the Sierra Nevada in California and Nevada," <u>Reports of the University of California Archaeological Survey</u>, No. 51. Berkeley: Department of Anthropology, University of California, 1960.

(14)   <u>Indians of California, Past and Present</u>, A report Prepared by American Friends Service Committee, 1850 Sutter Street, San Francisco, California, n.d.

(15)   Powers, Stephen, "Tribes of California," <u>Contributions to North American Ethnology, Department of the Interior, United States</u> <u>Geographical and Geological Survey of the Rocky Mountain Region, Vol. 3.</u> Washington, D.C.: United States Printing Office.

(16)   Riddell, Francis A. "Honey Lake Paiute Ethnography," <u>Nevada State Museum Anthropological Papers</u>, No. 4. Carson City, Nevada: Nevada State Museum, 1960.

(17)   Roseberry, Viola M. "Illustrated History of Indian Baskets and Plates Made by California Indians and Many Other Tribes," Published as a Souvenir for Lassen County Exhibit at 1915 Panama-Pacific-International Exposition, San Francisco, 1915. (Privately owned by local residents.)

(18)   Swartz, B.K. Jr. "A Study of the Material Aspects of Northeastern Maidu Basketry," <u>Reprint of the Kroeber Anthropological Society.</u> Berkeley: University of California Press, 1958.

PERIODICALS

(19)   Dixon, Roland B. "Basketry Designs of the Indians of Northern California," <u>Bulletin of the American Museum of Natural History</u>, Vol. 17, Part I, February 12, 1902, pp. 2-8; 11-14.

(20)   Dixon, Roland B. "Coyote Stories from the Maidu Indians," <u>Journal of American Folklore</u>, Vol. 13, pp. 267-70.

(21) Dixon, Roland B. "Maidu Myths," <u>Bulletin of the American Museum of Natural History</u>, Vol. 17, Part II, June 30, 1902, pp. 35-118.

(22) Dixon, Roland B. "Systems and Sequence in Maidu Mythology," <u>Journal of American Folklore</u>, Vol. 16, pp. 32-6.

(23) Dixon, Roland B. "The Northern Maidu," <u>Bulletin of the American Museum of Natural History</u>, Vol. 17, Part III, 1902, pp. 119-346.

(24) Hosselkus, John. "Remembrances of Genesee," <u>The Plumas County Historical Society Publication</u>, No. 4, April 9, 1961, pp. 26-9.

(25) Hosselkus, William R. "The Hosselkus Family," <u>The Plumas County Historical Society Publication</u>, No. 7, April 8, 1962, pp. 7-14.

(26) Young, Claude. "Taylorsville Tales," <u>The Plumas County Historical Society Publication</u>, No. 4, April 9, 1961, pp. 30-1.

NEWSPAPERS (broken files)

(27) <u>Greenville Bulletin</u>, October 6, 1880 – July 30, 1889.

(28) <u>Indian Valley Record</u>, November 21, 1930 – present.

(29) <u>Plumas Argus,</u> Quincy, September 17, 1857 – October 27, 1859.

(30) <u>Plumas Star</u>, Greenville, May 26, 1905 – October 22, 1909.

(31) <u>The Plumas National</u>, Quincy, August 18, 1866 – November 12, 1887.

(32) <u>The Plumas Standard</u>, Quincy, November 12, 1859 – February 7, 1863.

UNPUBLISHED MATERIALS

(33) Kurtz, John Cornell. "The Geology of the Indian Valley Region, Plumas County, California." Unpublished Master's thesis, Chico State College, Chico, California, 1957.

(34) McMillin, James Harold. "The Aboriginal Human Ecology of the Mountain Meadows Area in Southwestern Lassen County, California." Unpublished Master's thesis, Sacramento State College, Sacramento, California, 1963.

INDIAN INFORMANTS

(35) Baker, Bill. Residence, Lake Almanor, California. Northeastern Maidu. Age 48 years. Interviews 1958-63.

(36)   Baker, Daisy. Residence, Lake Almanor, California. Northeastern Maidu born at Prattville, California, May 6, 1879. Mother of Lilly and Bill Baker. Lived many years near Taylorsville and Genesee. Interviews 1958-63.

(37)   Baker, Lilly. Residence, Lake Almanor, California. Northeastern Maidu born near Taylorsville, California, July 6, 1911. Interviews 1958-63.

(38)   Davis, John. Residence Genesee, California. Northeastern Maidu born November 6, 1883. Interview April 1, 1963.

(39)   Davis, Otie. Residence, Genesee, C California. Northeastern Maidu born at Indian Mission, Indian Valley, California, July 19,1888. Interview April 1, 1963.

(40)   Young, Herbert. Residence, Oroville, California. Northeastern Maidu born at Genesee, California, May 124, 1892. Interviews 1958-63.

Information from informants of the Baker and Young families was gathered over a period of years and no definite date can be set as to when specific facts were given.

APPENDIX A

Maidu Names of places near and around Indian Valley, supplied by Herbert Young.

Villages

Si' lo	Village in Indian Valley
Kou' kok yakim	Village near Mel Gott ranch two miles from Greenville
Bu' nuk	Village between Rancheria and cemetery to the east
To ko chot	Village at mouth of Hunt Canyon
Waya' pom momi	Village north of Indian cemetery in Section 1
Ch' akom' duka	Village at Taylorsville Rancheria
Yetameto non	Village on rocky point, on right bank of Indian Creek below confluence of Grizzly Creek
Chilu' am in' komi	Village on the Johnson ranch between Crescent Mills and Taylorsville

Other Names

Ch'am sudono pakanin	Homer Lake
Ch' initbem yamaninom	Keddie Ridge
Elu' yem sewi	Clover Creek
Hope' nom	Area around Englemine
Koiyum bokum sewi'no	Indian Falls
Ko'tasim sewi	Wolf Creek
Ku'sim	Large hill in valley near Keddie Point
Tang ku' sim	Small hill in valley near Keddie Point
Ocho	Forgay Point

Om'yatatkim paka"nim	Taylor Lake
Pay' am yani	Mt. Jura
Pu' puwel' am say ween	Hosselkus Creek
Wa pan' beh'	Small hill on valley floor north of Taylorsville
Yeta' meto	Genesee Valley
Yetametom yamani	Wheeler Peak

Appendix B

THE DAWES ACT —- February 8, 1887. (from) Commager, Henry Steele (ed.), <u>Documents of American History</u>. New York: Appleton-Century-Crofts, Inc., 1958.

This act marked the end of a quarter of a century of agitation for reform in our treatment of the Indian problem. It was, said one philanthropist, "the end of a century of dishonor".

An act to provide for the allotment of land in severalty to Indians on the various reservations, and to extend the protection of the laws of the United States and the Territories over the Indians, and for other purposes.

Be it enacted, That in all cases where any tribes or bands of Indians has been, or shall hereafter be, located upon any reservation created for their use, either by treaty, stipulation or by virtue an act of Congress or executive order setting apart the same for their use, the President of the United States be, and he hereby is, authorized, whenever in his opinion any reservation or any part thereof of such Indian is advantageous for agriculture and grazing purposes to cause said reservation, or any part thereof, to be surveyed, or resurveyed if necessary and to allot the lands in said reservation in severalty to any Indian located thereon in quantities as follows:

To each head of a family, one quarter of a section;

To each single person over eighteen years of age, one-eighth of a section;

To each orphan child under eighteen years of age, one-eighth of a section; and

To each other single person under eighteen years now living, or who may be born prior to the date of this order of the President directing an allotment of the lands embraced in any reservation, one sixteenth of a section: ...

SEC. 5. That upon the approval of the allotments provided for in this act by the Secretary of the Interior, he shall ... declare that the land thus allotted, for the period of twenty-five years, in trust for the sole use and benefit of the Indian to whom such allotment shall have been made, ... and that at the expiration of said period the United States will convey the same by patent to said Indian, or his heirs as aforesaid, in fee, discharged of such trust and free of all charge or incumbrance whatsoever: ...

SEC. 6. That upon the completion of said allotments and the patenting of the lands to said allottees, each and every member of the respective bands or tribes of Indians to whom allotments have been made shall have the benefit of and be subject to the laws both civil and criminal, of the State or Territory in which they reside; ... And every Indian born within the territorial limits of the United States to whom allotments shall have been made under the provisions of this act, or under any law or treaty, and every Indian born within the territorial limits of the United States who has voluntarily taken up, within said limits, his residence separate and apart from any tribe of Indians therein, and has adopted the habits of civilized life, is hereby declared to be a citizen of the United States, and is entitled to all rights, privileges, and immunities of such citizens, whether said Indian has been or not, by birth or otherwise, a member of any tribe of Indians within the territorial limits of the United States without in any manner impairing or otherwise affecting the right of any such Indian to tribal or other property ...

UNITED STATES
DEPARTMENT OF THE INTERIOR
BUREAU OF INDIAN AFFAIRS

SACRAMENTO AREA OFFICE
P. O. BOX 749
SACRAMENTO, CALIFORNIA

IN REPLY REFER TO:

Tribal Operations
090

MAY 1 0 1963

Mrs. J. Cornell Kurtz
Box 357
Canyondam, California

Dear Mrs. Kurtz:

I regret the delay in replying to your April 5 letter requesting information about the Greenville Rancheria, Mission and school. A search of our files has not turned up data to answer all the seven questions asked in your letter.

We do not know when the school was actually established. The Women's National Indian Association, which was incorporated under the laws of the State of Pennsylvania, originally began the school as a day school and afterwards changed it to a boarding school, known as the Greenville Indian Industrial Boarding School. The United States acquired 40 acres of the school from the Women's National Indian Association on April 12, 1897. By Executive Order dated November 26, 1902, 160 acres was reserved and set aside for Indian school purposes and added to the existing acreage of the Greenville Indian School. Another 75 acres for a school farm was purchased on August 17, 1916.

As far as this office knows, the school was not for Maidu children only as when the Government operated schools for California Indian children, enrollment at a school was not restricted to a certain tribe. Our files do not show exactly when operation of the school was discontinued, but we believe it was in 1922, shortly after a fire destroyed the main school building. After the school was abandoned for such purposes, Maidu and other Indians of the general area used the land and it thus became a "rancheria" by reason of occupancy.

There are no enrollment or financial operation records or files for the school in this office. There are, however, some stored in the Federal Records Center in South San Francisco. Attached is a list of the files and Federal Record Center filing information. We believe it is possible for a private citizen to visit the Center and use the files for research purposes, but they cannot be removed from the Center.

We hope this information will be of some help to you.

Sincerely yours,

Maurice W. Babby
Acting Area Program Officer

Letter from: UNITED STATES DEPARTMENT OF THE INTERIOR, Bureau of Indian Affairs, Sacramento, California Area Office – May 10, 1963

Acknowledgement

If it were not for the encouragement and support of the following persons, this publication would not have been possible: Emi and Ken Holton, Tandy Bozeman, and George Thompson at the Meriam Library, Special Collections Department, California State University, Chico.